The Bible for Busy People

Book I: The Old Testament

Mark D. Berrier, Sr.

Seaside Press
an imprint of
Wordware Publishing, Inc.

Library of Congress Cataloging-in-Publication Data

Berrier, Mark D.
　　The Bible for busy people　/　Mark D. Berrier, Sr.
　　　　p.　　cm.
　　Includes index.
　　Contents: bk. 1. The Old Testament.
　　ISBN 1-55622-034-4 (v. 1)
　　1. Bible—Introductions.　I. Title.
　　BS475.2.B425　　1993　　　　　　　　　　93-36082
　　220.6'1—DC20　　　　　　　　　　　　　　CIP

ISBN 1-55622-032-4
10 9 8 7 6 5 4 3 2 1
9309

All inquiries for volume purchases of this book should be addressed to
Wordware Publishing, Inc., at the above address. Telephone inquiries may be
made by calling:

(214) 423-0090

Dedication and Acknowledgements

This book is dedicated to my Savior and Lord, Jesus Christ, the Son of God.

Thank You...

to Paula, my wife of 26 years, a gift from God. Without her love, encouragement, and commitment to me, this book would not exist.

to my parents, who first showed me God.

to Larry Cawood, brother, friend, elder. Without his hard work this book would not exist.

to Bobby Stephens for her computer work.

to Scott Binkley for his friendship. Our discussions and his constant questioning sharpen me. (Proverbs 27:17)

to Leroy Garrett, brother, friend, mentor, who gave me the title for this book.

to Ron Rife, for helping me accept myself.

to countless teachers, students, and friends, past and present, in whom also Christ is being formed. (Galatians 4:19)

to Dallas Christian College, its faculty and administration, who gave me the freedom to think, speak, and write.

to Valley View Church for their forgiveness and support.

to Harold Hampton, whose last words to me were, "Mark, teach them Jesus!"

Contents

Contents (Continued)

Preface

When people want to know Jesus Christ, they usually will go to church. They also become serious about studying the Bible. But this often doesn't help. Most sermons and Bible classes take for granted that people *already* know a lot about the Bible. When a friend of mine first became a Christian*, he kept hearing about Paul from his teachers and pastors*. He thought Paul must be another man in his church. He didn't know the Paul they talked about lived and served Jesus nearly 2,000 years ago. Nor did he know that this Paul wrote a lot of the Bible. My friend had never even read the Bible, let alone understood it!

So where should I start in a book like this? Let me first answer four questions:

1. What is the Bible?
2. What is the *Old Testament*?
3. What is the *New Testament*?
4. What is the *Gospel*?

The answers to these should give you a place to start from. Then you can begin your fascinating journey through the Bible.

1. *What is the Bible?* The Bible is a large book; in fact, it is a library of 66 books. It was written by at least 40 authors over a period of 1600 years. It was written in three languages—Hebrew, Aramaic, and Greek. The Bible is written to help bring us back to God.

2. *What is the Old Testament?* The *Old Testament** is the first 39 books of the Bible. It was first written in Hebrew and Aramaic. It tells the story of God creating the world, mankind's sin*, and God's actions to help us come back to him. The *Old Testament*

* Indicates words found in glossary.

contains *two major acts of God* after creation and sin: 1) God called one man, Abraham, to worship and obey him, and 2) God called one nation, Israel, to worship and obey him. Israel was to prepare for God's Son, who would come later to save all people. The one man, Abraham, began a family who finally became the great nation of Israel. Israel prepared the world for the coming of God's Son, Jesus Christ.

The *Old Testament* was put together in three parts: law, prophets, and writings; so the books are not in order like a history book.

3. **What is the New Testament?** The *New Testament** scriptures contain the story of *God's greatest work*—the life, death, and resurrection* of his Son, Jesus Christ. The first four books of the *New Testament* scriptures tell Jesus' story; the other twenty-three books tell what Jesus' story means to us. The first four books, Matthew, Mark, Luke, and John, are like a life story; the next book, Acts, tells of the start and growth of the early church; but the last twenty-two books were written to different people and churches to help them live as Christians, to live for Jesus.

The *New Testament* is actually our personal relationship with Jesus. (See II Corinthians 3 in the *New Testament* and Jeremiah 31:31-33 in the *Old Testament*.) The *New Testament* scriptures guide us in our relationship with Jesus as we grow up to become like him.

4. **What is the Gospel?**   The Gospel is *good news*: God has actually come into our world. He came into our time and space, in our history. He lived bodily in Jesus his son. After a sinless life, Jesus was murdered on the cross. He is the perfect sacrifice* to take away our sins*. He was taken down dead from the cross and was buried. He was raised on the third day to live forever to make us right with God. After Jesus' resurrection, He showed He was alive for many days. In the sight of His followers, He went up into heaven. Now He sits on the throne with God and pleads with God for us, so we are saved from hell. One day He will return. He will change us to be like Himself and take us home with Him. This is the Gospel; this is what Christians believe. Most of it is already done. We wait on the last part—Jesus' return. He is already our Savior; now let's let Him be our Lord, our Boss! We have been saved by what *He* has done; now, let's live it!

To the Reader:

Just as the Bible is different from other books, so our faith in God is different from all other religions of the world. *All* other religions are based on the thinking or private meditations of a man or men. Other religious writings contain these thoughts. NOT SO THE BIBLE. The Bible may contain men's thoughts, but faith is not based on thoughts or words. Our faith is based in history and in *acts*. Once an *act* is completed, it becomes a *fact* which nothing can ever change. So our faith is based in acts of history, not some human being's thoughts or ideas.

Teachings, thoughts, meditations may come and go, but the historical *facts* recorded in the Bible can never change! As in a court of law, *facts* make the case. As in a court of law, our faith is based on eyewitness accounts. Besides this, we have the miracle of predictions coming true, of fulfilled prophecies*. The Bible is believable, not because it is the thinking of a man, but because it is a record of facts which were seen and done out in the open. These facts are the work of God. There is, however, one WARNING:

A Warning to the Reader:

There is one thing you *must* avoid. You should not trust any group who believes that they alone have the truth. Any group who listens to only one leader or teacher, or any group who claims to be the only "true church," is dangerous. This is one of the marks of a *cult*—a group of people who allow no individual thinking, no freedom, and no differences of opinion. Avoid such groups. Instead, listen to more than one teacher; read everything you can. Then make your own decision to commit your life to Christ, totally, and find a Bible-believing, Bible-teaching church. Never stop studying and growing in your relationship with Christ; the Christian who stops growing dies. And always test what you hear, comparing it to what the Bible actually says. God's Holy Spirit, who lives in every Christian, will give you understanding.

Which Bible Should You Use?

Let's look briefly at the best-known Bible translations. Then you can choose the one which is best for your purpose.

NIV
: *New International Version*—If you are a good reader, and if your purpose is to *read* and *understand*, then the best translation is the *New International Version* (NIV). The NIV is an up-to-date translation into clear English. If, for instance, you decide to read the Gospel of Mark at one sitting, NIV is very helpful. The school where I teach uses the *NIV Study Bible*. It is great!

NAS
: *New American Standard Version*—If you want to *study* a section *in detail*, then the *New American Standard* (NAS) is best. The NAS is word-for-word and more accurate for study, especially when your NAS has "helps" in it. These helps give other possible meanings in footnotes. They also give cross-references, which list other places in the Bible where the same word or idea may be found.

It is better when studying the Bible to use several translations. Here are some others you could use:

KJV
: *King James Version*—Completed by Anglican scholars in England in 1611, this is an out-dated version, very hard now for most people to read and understand.

NKJ
: *New King James*—An up-to-date edition of the old version, it is quite accurate for the most part.

TEV
: *Today's English Version* (also called *The Good News Bible*)—A simple, clear, new translation, originally made for people who know English only as a second language. It is limited to an 800-word vocabulary. It is very readable, good especially for children, but helpful for anyone. It is for *reading*, not *studying*.

NEB
: *New English Bible*—A high-class, rather intellectual translation for people who know the English language well.

RSV   *Revised Standard Version*—This is the one that I studied originally, before I learned the Greek and Hebrew languages. Generally, it is on about the same level as the NAS. (See above.)

Phl.   *Phillips*—A well-done, modern paraphrase of the *New Testament* that can be very helpful.

LB   *Living Bible*—A helpful Bible when you're just reading to get an overall view of a passage. Not a good study Bible.

JB   *Jerusalem Bible*—This compares with NAS mentioned above. It is a scholarly translation with helpful footnotes.

ICB   *International Children's Bible*—An excellent, very simple translation. It is for a person who has trouble reading or who doesn't like to read.

There are other translations which may be helpful, too, but your best choices are probably the NIV, NAS, *Today's English Version*, or the *International Children's Bible*.

Conclusion:—If this is your first time to read the Bible, I suggest *Today's English Version* (TEV). It is a very simple translation. However, if you are a better than average reader, you could use the *New International Version* (NIV).

When you are not just reading the Bible, but want to *study* it, then compare several different versions. This may give you a clearer picture of what is being said.

The Plan of This Book

The following order is used in the chapters of this book:

1. A short summary of each book, beginning with Genesis;

2. A brief outline of each book;

3. A brief, clear, simple overview of each *Old Testament* book, including important or best-known key verses that help us to understand that book;

4. Exciting points of interest or special studies that apply to us as we grow to be like Jesus.

Helps in reading this book:

1. The first time an unusual word or name appears in the book an asterisk or star (*) is placed after it. These words are in the glossary at the back of the book. For example, asterisk is a word you can look up in the glossary.

2. As you read, you will sometimes see †. This tells you about a special study. These special studies are at the end of each chapter. They are marked 1, 2, etc. These special studies are called "Lessons from ..."

3. Scriptures are listed in the order of book, chapter, and verse. For example, Genesis 1:1 means the book of Genesis, chapter 1, verse 1.

4. Sometimes an "f" or "ff" follows the book, chapter, and verse. If you see "f," it means one verse following; if you see "ff" it means more verses following. For example, Genesis 1:1f means verses 1 and 2; Genesis 1:1ff means more than two verses.

GENESIS

SUMMARY OF GENESIS

Genesis is the first book of the Bible. Genesis means *beginning.* God created the world. People sinned. God destroyed all but Noah and seven others in the flood. God called Abraham*. Abraham believed God. God blessed* Abraham and his family—Isaac, then Jacob*, then Joseph. Joseph brought everyone in Jacob's family into Egypt. Jacob died, then Joseph died. So Genesis ends with all the family of Jacob in Egypt.

OUTLINE

  A. Early history before Abraham (Genesis 1-11)
  1. Creation and sin* (Genesis 1-5)
  2. The flood (Genesis 6-9)
  3. The tower and the nations (Genesis 10-11)

  B. Abraham and the early fathers (patriarchs*) (Genesis 12-50)
  1. Abraham and Isaac (Genesis 12:1-25:18)
  2. Jacob (Genesis 25:19-36)
  3. Joseph (Genesis 37-50)

OVERVIEW

Genesis shows us the beginning of everything. God created the universe in a special order. He made people last of all, as the crown of all God's creation. He put Adam and Eve in a beautiful place and asked them to take care of it. The only rule was, "Do not eat fruit from the tree of the knowledge of good and evil or you'll die." (Genesis 2:17) But Adam and Eve were quick to eat from that tree, even though there were many others good to eat from. They ate because a talking snake lied to Eve. He said, "If you eat, you won't die; you will be like God."[†1] (Genesis 3:4f) The snake was Satan. (Our world today is full of sickness, evil, and death, because Adam and Eve listened to Satan's lie.) When God came to Adam and Eve, they hid. They were afraid of God because of their sin. God put a curse on the snake, then he put a curse on the ground (Genesis 3:14, 17). He told Eve that she would have great pain when she had children. He told Adam that he would have great pain in his work. He would have to work hard as a farmer to live; and one day, they would die. In those days, though, most people lived nearly 1,000 years! (See Genesis 5.)

Adam and Eve had many children, and their children had many children. Cain and Abel were born to Adam and Eve. Both boys grew up and worshipped God, but Cain didn't really believe and obey God (Genesis 4:2-5 and see in the *New Testament** Hebrews 11:4 and I John 3:12). Cain became angry and murdered Abel.[†2] God punished Cain, but even then put a mark of protection on Cain, so no one would murder him (Genesis 4:15).

But people became more and more evil (Genesis 6:5). So God chose to save eight—Noah, his wife, his three sons, and their wives. God told Noah to build a huge box called an ark. "I will send rain on the earth," God said. So Noah built the ark with his sons' help. It was big enough for Noah, his family, and many animals to live inside. When Noah was done, God sent the eight people and some land animals into the ark; then he sent a great flood on the earth. Everyone on earth except Noah's family died. All land animals died except those on the ark. After more than a year, the flood waters went down. The ark landed on Ararat Mountain in northern Turkey. God had saved some animals and eight people to start the world again.

Noah's family began to have more and more children. Everyone in the world spoke one simple language. They all decided to build one giant city with a tower that would reach toward heaven. But God didn't want everyone in one place, so he made them speak different languages. Since they couldn't understand each other any more, they had to quit working on the city. Then they began to scatter all over the world.†3

Abraham and Isaac: In Genesis 12 God began his plan to call people back to himself—he called Abraham to follow him. Abraham lived in Ur*, among people who were evil. They worshipped idols and false gods, like the moon, the sun, or the stars. God called him to leave the city where he lived and become a traveller who lived in a tent.

God gave Abraham three promises: 1) he would be the father of a nation; 2) the nation would have its own land; and 3) all the peoples on earth would be blessed through Abraham. (See Genesis 12:1-3.) So Abraham went. God appeared to him and talked to him several times. He promised Abraham, "You will have a son."

"Abraham believed God, and God counted Abraham right with him." (Genesis 15:6) This is the first time the Bible *says* that God accepted someone because of his faith*. Abraham believed in God's promise of a son for twenty-five years before Isaac was born. Abraham first believed the promise when he was seventy-five years old; the promise was kept twenty-five years later, when Abraham was 100. When Abraham was ninety-nine years old, God had commanded him to be circumcised*. So Abraham was circumcised and all the men of his house were circumcised. This was the outward sign of God's covenant* with Abraham.

Ishmael was a half-brother to Isaac, about thirteen years older than Isaac. But he was not the promised son; he was a slave's child, even though Abraham was his father.†4

When Isaac was a young man, God told Abraham to kill Isaac and burn him up as a sacrifice. God did this to test Abraham's faith. Abraham got up early and led Isaac away on a three-day journey. He took two slaves with him, too. When they got to Moriah Mountain, the mountain God had chosen, Abraham told the slaves to wait. He said, "My son and I will go up there and worship; then we will return to you." At the top of the hill, Isaac let Abraham tie him up on the altar.

Under him, the wood was on fire. Abraham raised the knife to kill Isaac, but the Lord* called to him and told him not to hurt Isaac. God knew that Abraham trusted him totally. So Abraham looked up and saw a male sheep caught in some thorns. He exchanged Isaac for the sheep and offered the sheep instead.†5

Abraham's wife, Sarah, died, so Abraham bought some property in Southern Palestine* near the city of Hebron* where he buried her body. Then he sent a slave to his old home country of Ur to get a wife for Isaac. Beautiful Rebekah returned with the slave and married forty-year-old Isaac. Then Abraham died, 175 years old.

Jacob: At first, Isaac's life was not very interesting. Rebekah had no children for some time, so Isaac prayed for her. Then she had twins. The twins were Jacob and Esau*. Now their lives were interesting! Esau was born first, so he received the birthright*. Jacob grew up to be a "mama's boy" who liked to do the housework; Esau was a hunter—"a man's man." Jacob took Esau's birthright away from him by tricking him. (See Genesis 25:29-34.) Then Jacob had to trick his old blind father, Isaac, to get his blessing*. His mother, Rebekah, helped him. (See Genesis 27.) So Jacob stole Isaac's best blessing, the promise God had given to Abraham. (Compare Genesis 12:1-3 and 27:29.) Esau was angry. Jacob was afraid Esau would kill him, so he ran away. He went to his grandfather Abraham's home country, Ur, in Messopotamia*.

On his way to Messopotamia, Jacob had a dream about a ladder. God appeared to him and renewed Abraham's promise to Jacob. (See Genesis 28:13-15.) Jacob bargained with God—"If you will protect me on my trip, and take care of my needs, then I will serve you." (Compare Genesis 28:20-22.) So Jacob arrived at his uncle Laban's* house. He worked for Laban and was tricked by Laban again and again. He married Laban's two daughters, Leah and Rachel, and their two slaves. From his two wives and two concubines* he had several sons. Each son later became the father of a great tribe of people. (These were called "the twelve tribes of Israel.")

Jacob decided to leave Laban after several years. He waited until Laban was working far from home. Then he loaded all his people and things and took off, driving his herds of animals with him. Unknown to Jacob, Rachel had stolen Laban's "household idols"* and hidden them. Laban found out they had left, and he chased after Jacob. The night before Laban caught up with Jacob, God warned Laban not to hurt him. So Laban let Jacob and all his family and property get away. (See Genesis 31.)

Now Jacob *really* was afraid! He was about to meet Esau, the older brother, the warrior, the one he first cheated out of his birthright. But God's angels met him so he wouldn't be too afraid (Genesis 32:1). Jacob sent gifts of cattle and slaves to Esau, and he sent his family on ahead, across a stream called Jabbok*. That night God came to Jacob, and they wrestled together all night long (Genesis 32:22-32). It was here God changed Jacob's name to Israel. Next morning, Jacob was a changed man! Esau forgave him, and he settled in Palestine with all his family. He lived in the place where he had the dream of the ladder, Bethel*. Rachel died near Bethel. She died giving birth to Jacob's twelfth son, Benjamin. (The twelve sons are named in Genesis 35:23-26.)

Joseph was Jacob's eleventh son, his favorite son (Genesis 37). Joseph was a dreamer. He dreamed that his brothers and his mother and father would all bow down to him. His brothers hated him for it. They planned to kill him. Instead, one day they sold him to some of their cousins in a caravan on the way to Egypt. Then they dipped his coat in sheep's blood and showed it to Jacob, their father. Jacob was heartbroken. Joseph had been his favorite son. So the family pretty much forgot about Joseph, the brothers in guilt and Jacob in grief. But Joseph was still alive in Egypt. He was slave to a high-ranking Egyptian leader named Potiphar. Joseph was a very helpful slave, but he was so good-looking that Potiphar's wife wanted to have sex with him. Day after day she kept asking him to go to bed with her. He would not do it, so she lied to Potiphar. She said, "Joseph tried to rape me!" In anger, Potiphar threw him in prison. But even there, Joseph was a good slave, so the jailer made him a leader in the prison. The Lord was with Joseph in whatever he did.

Two men in prison had dreams (Genesis 40). With God's help, Joseph was able to tell what their dreams meant. One man would be taken out of jail and put back in the king's service. The other would be killed. When the dreams came true, Joseph was forgotten in prison. But two years later, the king had two dreams. No one could tell what they meant. Then the prisoner who had been freed and who was now working for the king remembered Joseph! Joseph was cleaned up and taken to the king. With God's help, he told the king the meaning of his dreams—there would be seven years of much food, then seven years of no food. So the king put Joseph in charge of storing up the food. He filled every storage place with food. Then came the seven years of no food. Everyone in the world came to Egypt, to Joseph, for food. Finally, even Joseph's brothers ran out of food in Palestine, and they came to Egypt for food. They didn't know who Joseph was when they saw him, but he knew them. It had been at least twenty years since they had seen each other, probably longer. (See Genesis 37:2 and 41:46; thirteen years plus seven years of much food, at least.)

Joseph treated them badly, scared them, and tricked them. They went home with food, afraid, because Joseph had their money put in with their food. When they ran out of food, they had to go back again. This time Joseph gave them their food and his favorite silver cup. Egypt's army went after them and brought them back to Joseph. This time Joseph couldn't control himself. He broke down and cried. Then he told them who he was. They were terrified of him, thinking he would pay them back for selling him into slavery. But he told them to get their father, Jacob (or Israel), and come to Egypt to live.

So all his family went into Egypt, into the upper Nile River area, to the best land in Egypt. With the king's permission, Joseph gave this land, the Land of Goshen, to his family. And that is how the tribe of Israel got into Egypt.

Later, Jacob (now called Israel) blessed his sons and grandsons, and then he died. The best blessing he gave to Judah*, because Jesus Christ would one day be born out of this tribe. (See Genesis 49:8-12.)

When their father Jacob died, the brothers were really afraid. Again, they thought Joseph would get even with them for selling him into slavery. They thought Joseph would kill them, because their father was now dead. But Joseph said, "You meant it for evil, but God meant it for good." So God's plan was begun. One of his prophecies of the future was fulfilled. (See Genesis 15:13.) The people of Israel were living in a foreign land—Egypt. Joseph died, and he was put in a box in Egypt. But his family had promised him they would take him out of Egypt when they left. They also promised to bury him in Canaan*, their future home country.

LESSONS FROM GENESIS

†1 — *Satan's Word*: He told Adam and Eve, "You will not die." This was the first lie. But whenever Satan tempts us, he tells the same lie. He always says, "Go ahead. One time won't hurt you." He always *denies the penalty for sin.* He tells the drunk, "You won't get cirrhosis* of the liver." He tells the homosexual, "You won't get AIDS." He tells the smoker, "You won't get cancer." And so on. Sin *always* has a penalty.

†2 — *Cain and Abel*: Before Cain killed Abel, God told him that sin was like a lion, crouching near the door, and that sin wanted to destroy Cain. God said, "You must overcome sin!" (Genesis 4:7) But Cain didn't overcome it. Instead, sin overcame Cain. It is easier to overcome sin when you are young, with God's help. As we get older, sin becomes harder and harder to overcome.

†3 — *The city, Babel*: God knew that if people kept the same language, if they stayed together and built the city, they would become as evil as they were before the flood. (See Genesis 6:5.) The first big city described in the Bible is Sodom. (See Genesis 19:1-29.) It was filled with sin. If the tower and city of Genesis 11 had been built, people would have been united in evil.

†4 — *Abraham and Ishmael*: In the old days, if a woman could not have children, she could give her female slave to her husband. That way, the slave could have children, but the children belonged to the slave-owner who could not have children. Ishmael was born this way. Abraham had sex with his wife's Egyptian slave, whose name was Hagar. When Hagar had the baby, Ishmael, she made fun of Sarah, her owner, because Sarah couldn't have children. Ishmael made fun of Isaac, too, later on, because he was bigger, older, and stronger than Isaac. To this day, Ishmael's family, the Arabs, are a problem to Isaac's family, the Jews!

†5 — *Abraham and Isaac*: Genesis 22 is an interesting story. God is Jesus' father, yet he still let Jesus die. In the same way, God asked Abraham

to kill Isaac as an offering. Their trip to Moriah Mountain is three days long, so in Abraham's mind his son is "dead" for three days. When they got there, Abraham put the wood for the sacrifice altar on Isaac's back, just as Jesus had to carry his own cross. When they left the slaves at the foot of the mountain, Abraham said ". . . we will return to you." That means Abraham believed God would raise Isaac from the dead, as he did Jesus. So Abraham's faith is really like ours: We believe in the virgin birth of Jesus; he believed (1) in the miracle birth of Isaac, (Genesis 15:6 and Romans 4:19-21) and (2) he believed in resurrection* of the dead, (Hebrews 11:19 and Romans 4:17) just as we do. Genesis ends about 1,900 years before Jesus was born (nearly 4,000 years ago!).

EXODUS

SUMMARY OF EXODUS

(Date of events: about 1560-1440 B.C.) In Genesis you learned how the people of Israel got into Egypt. About 400 years passed. Then in Exodus you learn how God led the people of Israel out of Egypt. Exodus is the fulfillment of God's first promise to Abraham: Israel is now a *nation*.

Exodus means *the way out*, like the word *exit*. Moses* is the main writer of Exodus. As Abraham, then Jacob, then Joseph were the main actors in Genesis, Moses is the main actor in Exodus. Really, in all these books, the *main* actor is God.

Exodus begins about 1,560 years before Jesus' birth and ends about 1,400 years before his birth. So the book covers about 160 years. Moses lived 120 of those years.

The Israelites were slaves in Egypt. Moses was chosen by God to free the Israelites. God sent plagues on the Egyptians. Israel went out. God opened the Red Sea, and Israel crossed on dry land. God destroyed Egypt's army. Israel went to Sinai where God gave them the Ten Commandments.

OUTLINE

A. God took Israel out of Egypt (Exodus 1-15)

    a. Israel, a great nation, are slaves in Egypt (1)

    b. Moses is sent to lead Israel out (2-6)

    c. God sends terrible pain on Egypt: the ten plagues (7-11)

9

OVERVIEW

A new king took over Egypt. He knew nothing about Joseph, and he was afraid because the Israelites had become so many. So he made them slaves and even tried to kill their boy babies. When this was going on, Moses was born. His parents kept him hidden for awhile, but finally they couldn't hide him anymore. So they made a little boat and put Moses in it. He floated away down the Nile River. The princess of Egypt found him, and she raised him as her own son.

When Moses grew up, he killed an Egyptian who was beating an Israelite, and he had to run away from Egypt. He lived out in the desert for about forty years. One day God called him from a desert bush that was on fire but was not burning up. He told Moses to go to Egypt and free the people of Israel. He even gave Moses some miracles to do, to prove God had sent him.[t1] He sent Aaron*, his brother, with him.

Moses did what God wanted. God sent terrible plagues on Egypt each time the king of Egypt refused to let Israel go. Moses warned the king over and over, but the king would not listen. So God finally passed over Egypt (this is where the name *Passover* came from). The people of Israel had put lamb's blood over their doors because God had said, "When I see the blood, I will pass over you." But the Egyptians had no lamb's blood over their doors, so God killed the oldest son in every Egyptian's house. All Egypt cried over their dead. They gave gold and silver to the Israelites and begged them to leave their land. So, about 1,440 years before Jesus was born, Moses led Israel out of Egypt. There were probably over two million Israelites who left with Moses. Israel had been in Egypt over 400 years.

When all Israel got to the Red Sea, they stopped. They were caught between the Red Sea and the whole Egyptian army! The king of Egypt was angry. He sent the army after them, and the Israelites were afraid. But God went behind them and protected Israel with fire all night long. God parted the Red Sea, and Israel crossed the sea on dry land. The next day the Egyptians chased Israel, but when they got into the middle of the Red Sea, God let it close up over them. Egypt's army was drowned, but the Israelites were safe in the desert. In the desert God gave the people manna (miracle food) and miracle drink. (Exodus 16-17)

Then Moses led them to Sinai Mountain where there was lightning, thunder, and a terrible dark cloud. All Israel was terrified, but Moses went up the mountain. There, God gave Moses the Ten Commandments plus rules for proper worship. (Exodus 21-40)

Moses was up on the mountain forty days. During that time the Israelites went back to their bad Egyptian habits of worshiping idols. They made a gold calf. Then they had a wild party and were very evil. When he saw them, Moses was so angry that he threw down the stone tablets that the Ten Commandments were written on. God punished the idol worshippers with a plague, and Moses had to go back up the mountain for forty more days to get the Ten Commandments again. The rest of Exodus is a record of all the rules for Israel and for their worship.

LESSONS FROM EXODUS

[†1] — God did these miracles in Exodus:

1. The bush that burned without burning up (3:1ff)
2. The leprous* hand healed (4:6-7)
3. The stick that became a snake (4:2-5 and 7:10-13)
4. The water turned to blood (7:14-24)
5. The frogs (7:25-8:15)
6. The gnats or maggots (8:16-19)
7. The flies (8:20-23)
8. The cattle sickness (9:1-7)
9. The boils (9:8-12)

10. The hail (9:13-35) (Even rain in Egypt was very rare; hail was unheard of.)
11. The locusts (10:1-20)
12. The darkness for three days (10:29-32)
13. The death of Egypt's oldest sons (12:29-32)
14. The pillar of fire and smoke (from 13:21 on. See especially 40:34-38)
15. Walking on dry land through the Red Sea (14 and 15)
16. Bitter water turned sweet (15:22-25)
17. Manna* (16) (The manna rotted overnight—except on the Sabbath*.)
18. Quail (16:12-13)
19. Water from the Rock (17:1-8)
20. Cloud, thunder, lightning, trumpets, earthquake at Sinai (19)
21. The giving of the law (20ff)
22. Moses and the leaders of Israel *saw* God (24:9-11)
23. Moses' face glowed brightly (34:29-35)

People are always amazed that Israel could see all these miracles and still not believe. God did all the great plagues in Egypt; he led and protected the people at the Red Sea; he even blew the sea apart so they could cross on dry land; he fed them the "bread of heaven" (manna) and let them drink water from the Rock. (See I Corinthians 10:1-4 in the *New Testament* and Exodus 17:1-7.) But most of the people did not believe. That is why most of them died in the desert!

Jesus said to his enemies (John 7:28), "You know me and you know where I am from...". But his enemies still would not *believe* in him. It is possible to *know* but not *believe*. *Knowing* is mental; *believing* is in our hearts! We can know something we don't *want* to know, but we can't believe unless we *choose* to believe! (See John 7:16-17.)

LEVITICUS

SUMMARY OF LEVITICUS

(Date of events: about 1440 B.C.) In Exodus you learned how God led the Israelites out of Egypt. In Leviticus you learn about the rules for God's priests* and for Israel.

Leviticus means *belonging to the Levites**. Moses is the main writer of Leviticus. The main actors in the book are the priests, Moses, and God. The main idea in Leviticus is God's holiness* and how people have to be holy* to be God's friends. The book tells of all the rules needed to be holy under the *Old Testament* Law. Sacrifices and priests and people had to be perfect to really worship God. This is why animal sacrifices were needed . . . to show people the awfulness of sin before a Holy God.

OUTLINE

A. Five kinds of *perfect* offerings (Leviticus 1-7):
   1. Burnt offering of animals (1)
   2. Offering of grain (2)
   3. Offering of animals for peace and sharing (3)
   4. Offering of animals or grain for accidental sin (4)
   5. More discussion of sins and offerings (5-7), including the "guilt offering" (5:14-6:7)

B. Other rules (Leviticus 8-27):

   1. The priests' work (8-10)

   2. Laws about worship and the tabernacle* (16, 17)

   3. More rules (18-25)

   4. Why Israelites must obey (26)

   5. Rules about keeping promises to the Lord (27)

OVERVIEW

God called certain men to be priests. He gave them the rules in Leviticus so they would know *how* to offer the sacrifices that God wanted. All the sacrifices and rules in the book show us how hard it would be to *work* enough and be *perfect* enough to please God. Even with all these rules, no one could be good enough to please God. This is why God saves us by our faith and his grace! We could never do enough or be good enough to be like God. This was the reason for sacrificing the animals. Every sin must result in a death. This is why Jesus had to die, as the *New Testament* scriptures tell us. His death blots out our sins if we believe and follow him. As God said in Exodus, "When I see the blood, I will pass over you." But now it's Jesus' blood. We believe in him, so his blood cleans us from all sin.

More important than all the rules and the work of the priests is one part of a verse in Leviticus: "Love your neighbor as yourself." All laws are summed up in those five words. They are repeated at least nine times in the *New Testament*. If we treat others as we wish they would treat us, we fulfill all the laws.

LESSONS FROM LEVITICUS

†1 — People must be pure enough to worship God. God gave Moses and Aaron and the priests rules to follow, so people could *try* to be pure. Leviticus is a book of rules for priests and people. Leviticus makes me glad of one thing: only the blood of Jesus really purifies us. Thank God for his Son!

NUMBERS

SUMMARY OF NUMBERS

(Date of events: about 1440-1400 B.C.) In Leviticus you learned about rules for priests and people. In Numbers you learn about Israel's years wandering in the desert, as God gets them ready to enter the promised land.

The book is called *Numbers* because it begins with a census; Moses counts the people of Israel at Sinai Mountain. Again, Moses is the main character and main writer of this book. Numbers covers some of the same events as Exodus.

OUTLINE

A. Israel at Sinai (1:1-10:10)

B. From Sinai to Kadesh (10:11-20:13)

C. From Kadesh to Moab* (20:14-25:18)

D. Getting ready to enter the promised land (26-36)

OVERVIEW

First in the book, Israel's army was counted[†1]. There were way over one-half million able-bodied men who were twenty years old or older in the army. (See Numbers 1:45 and 46.) Levi's tribe of priests were not counted. Counting women, children, the old, and the young, there had to be at least two million Israelites in the desert. God organized them into a mighty army under his command.

God wanted his people to be pure and holy, so he gave more rules to purify them. Among the rules is the Nazarite* vow* (Numbers 6) and the priestly blessing: "God bless and keep you; God be happy with you and bless you; God watch over you and give you peace!"

Israel celebrated the passover again in the desert of Sinai. (See Numbers 9:1-14.) Then they left Sinai and followed God in the pillar of cloud. Much of Numbers is like our study of Exodus. The Israelites rebelled against God over and over[+2]. Even Moses' brother Aaron and sister Miriam rebelled. God gave Miriam leprosy* but later healed her. The people of Israel kept making God angry by their complaining and rebelling. (Some people say "Numbers" should be named "Complaining" instead.)

Moses chose twelve men to look over the promised land, to see if Israel should move up north and attack the cities of Canaan. They explored the land, but ten of the twelve said Israel should not attack Canaan, because the people of the land were too great and strong. They forgot that God was with them! The other two men, Joshua* and Caleb, said Israel should attack Canaan. But the Israelites didn't believe Joshua and Caleb; instead, they rebelled again against God. (See Numbers 14.) This is why Israel had to wander around in the desert for forty years. (See Numbers 14:34.) God wanted to wait until all the unbelieving people died. He would let them attack Canaan later, with Joshua and Caleb as leaders. (See Numbers 14:29 and 30.)

Among the unbelievers who died in the desert were some who died by fire from the Lord (Numbers 3:4, 11:1-3 and 16:35); at least one was stoned to death for breaking God's rule about no work on the Sabbath Day (15:32-36); Korah, Dathan, Abiram, and their followers were killed by an earthquake caused by God (16:31 and 32); others were killed by a plague of poisonous snakes (21:4-9); others were killed by other plagues (for example, see Numbers 14:36-38); and many died of other causes.

Israel fought some of the desert kingdoms and beat them. This made Balak, king of Moab, afraid. So he sent for a true prophet* of God named Balaam to prophesy* against Israel. Balak wanted Balaam to curse Israel. Balak offered Balaam enough money to buy his obedience, even though God told Balaam not to go. An angel* stood in the path to kill Balaam. Balaam couldn't see the angel, but the donkey he rode saw him. The animal turned aside twice to avoid the angel and finally lay down under Balaam in fear of the angel. When Balaam began to beat the donkey, God made the donkey *speak* to Balaam! Then Balaam knew the donkey had saved his life. (See Numbers 22:21ff.)

He went on to prophesy for Balak, but instead of cursing Israel, he blessed them. Balak was angry, but God had no plans to attack Moab anyway, because Moabites* are kin to Israel. (To learn how Moab and Israel are related, see Genesis 19:30-38. Lot was Abraham's nephew.)

Israel took another census of all the army. It counted over 600 thousand able-bodied men again, even though so many of the older ones had died. More rules and laws were given to get the Israelites ready to enter the promised land. Israel conquered more desert kingdoms. They completed their forty years of wandering. Then God told them how the promised land was to be divided among them. Joshua took over for Moses. Now the Israelites were ready to enter the land.

The Israelites were counted at the beginning and at the end of the forty years of wandering in the desert. God fed them manna and quail for the whole time; he gave them water to drink from the desert Rock[3]. But the people complained and rebelled; so God made them keep wandering, until the young ones replaced the old ones. Then God blessed them and made them ready for their new home during those forty years.

LESSONS FROM NUMBERS

[1] — *The numbers of Numbers*: The exact number of Israel's army is in Numbers 1:45 and 46, which was 603,550 soldiers. These were at least twenty years old and could serve as soldiers. It omits all who were ill or crippled or Levites. (The priests were not soldiers.) This means that the seventy Israelites who entered Egypt had multiplied very quickly. Jacob himself had twelve sons and a daughter by four women. Then there would have been twelve to sixteen generations in the 400 years they were in Egyptian slavery. Some experts guess

that there were really somewhere between two and four million Israelites in the desert. No wonder the king of Egypt was so afraid of them! (See Exodus 1:8-10 and 1:16 where the king even tells them to kill all baby boys.) Imagine God's power, being able to feed all those mouths every day for forty years!

†2 — *Death for the Rebels*: God caused the death of all the rebels, gripers, and unbelievers in the desert. Only Joshua and Caleb from that generation entered the promised land. That means over 600 thousand people died in the desert. That is a picture of what God is doing for us. We believe in Jesus, and we are baptized; that is how we die! Read Romans 6:3, 4, and 8 in the *New Testament*. We die here (by faith and baptism) so we can enter our promised land—heaven.

†3 — *Water from the Rock*: In the *Old Testament* God is often called a "Rock." (See Psalms* 18:2; 31:3; 42:9 and Deuteronomy 32:15 among others.) In the *New Testament* Jesus is often called the Rock. I Corinthians 10:1-13 is a summary of Exodus and Numbers. It tells of crossing the Red Sea, the pillar of cloud or fire, the manna, and drinking from the Rock. There, the scriptures say "that Rock was Christ!" Moses hit the Rock, and the water gushed out. In the same way, Jesus had to be "hit" (beaten, killed, and raised again) for the Holy Spirit to be given. So the Rock is like Christ and the water is like the Holy Spirit. (Read John 7:37-39.)

DEUTERONOMY

SUMMARY OF DEUTERONOMY

(Date of events: about 1400 B.C.) Deuteronomy is a series of sermons spoken by Moses in about 1400 B.C., just before Israel entered the promised land.

In Numbers you learned about Israel's desert wanderings, as God was getting them ready for their new home. Deuteronomy is a review of all that happened in Egypt and the desert. Also, Moses gave warnings (curses) and promises (blessings) for the future in the promised land.

Moses delivered three sermons to renew the covenant between God and Israel. They learned that if they obeyed, they would be happy; if they disobeyed, they would be miserable. Moses died and Joshua took over.

OUTLINE

A. Review of Exodus and Numbers (1-4)

B. The Ten Commandments and the greatest commandment (4-6)

C. Review of History and Laws (7-26)

D. Keep the Law to be blessed; disobey God to be cursed (27-30)

E. Joshua takes Moses' place; Moses blesses the people (31-33)

F. Moses' death (34)

OVERVIEW

Deuteronomy means *second law*. It is a review of God's law and his agreement with all Israel. In the Bible, this "agreement" is called a *covenant*. Moses wanted to renew this covenant between God and Israel. He wanted the people of Israel to be totally committed to God and to obey him. He spoke these things forty years after the law was given at Sinai. Nearly all the older generation had died, and Moses was about to die.

In Deuteronomy, Moses reviewed the first four books of the Bible, reminding the Israelites of God's promises to Abraham, Isaac, and Jacob. He asked the people to renew their commitment and their obedience to the Lord. He renewed the covenant with all its promises. If they obey, God will bless them. If they do not obey the law, they will be very unhappy until they die.

The Ten Commandments were given again, as in Exodus 20. The difference this time is that Moses gives them and tells what they mean. (See Deuteronomy 5.) But the one greatest commandment is: "Listen, Israel! The Lord our God is One! You must love him with all you are and all you have!" The religion of the *Old Testament* is based on careful listening and then doing what we hear. Listen. Obey. Love God[1]. (See Deuteronomy 6:4ff.)

Near the end of Deuteronomy, Joshua took over. In chapter 34, God showed Moses the great promised land from a mountain in Moab. Then Moses died and God buried him.

LESSONS FROM DEUTERONOMY

[1] — Loving God may seem like a hard thing to do for some people. But in the *New Testament*, Jesus said that to love God you must' love people. (See Matthew 22:37-40.) Jesus said that *all* of the *Old Testament* depends on these two things: Love God and love people. So all ten commandments are summed up in *love*. And love means helping others.

The first five commandments are vertical; that is, they point up to God. (See the list in Exodus 20 or Deuteronomy 5.) The last five commandments are horizontal; that is, they point to other people. So we are to serve people; that is how we can serve God. Jesus said, "If you do it for the least of my brothers, you do it for *me*." (See Matthew 25:40 and context*.)

JOSHUA

SUMMARY OF JOSHUA

(Date of Events: about 1410-1360 B.C.) In Deuteronomy you learned about the renewal of the covenant between God and Israel. In Joshua you see God's second promise to Abraham fulfilled: Israel gets its own land. (See Genesis 12:1-3.)

Israel entered Canaan and began to conquer it. They divided up the land among the tribes as God had told them. After they were settled in their new land, Joshua died. Before he died he renewed the covenant between God and Israel again. (See Joshua 23 and 24.)

OUTLINE

1. Israel enters the promised land (1-5)

2. Israel conquers the land (6-12)

3. Israel divides up the land among its tribes (13-22)

4. Joshua's final words (23-24)

OVERVIEW

Joshua is the record of Israel's invasion of Canaan. The book is named after Joshua, its most important character. It was Joshua who took over for Moses and led the people into the promised land. After over 400 years in Egypt and forty years in the desert, the people of Israel were finally ready and able to enter the land God had promised to them. The

Book of Joshua follows logically after the first five books of Moses. Much of the book was written by Joshua, but the last chapter was written later, by someone else. It tells of Joshua's death.

Jericho was the gateway city into Canaan. (See map of Canaan.) So Joshua sent two spies into Jericho. The people of the land were terrified. They knew the Israelites were coming and that God was with Israel. Rahab was a prostitute in Jericho. She protected the two spies, because she believed in the Lord. So the spies promised to protect her and her family when Israel invaded the land.

When the people were ready to cross the Jordan River, it was during its flood time. But according to God's word, the priests carrying God's covenant box* stepped into the river. The river stopped flowing! Instead, the water piled up to the north. (This is similar to the Red Sea crossing. See Exodus 14:21-31.) The people walked across on dry land. When the people saw this miracle, they respected Joshua the same way they had respected Moses.

They camped near Jericho at Gilgal. The people of Jericho were afraid, so the city's gates were closed and locked. Five things happened on the plain near Jericho: 1) all the Israelite men were circumcised; 2) the people celebrated the Passover; 3) they ate food from their new land; 4) the manna stopped; 5) Joshua met and worshipped "the commander of the Lord's army[†1]." It was time to attack Jericho. God had a very strange way of doing it. They marched around Jericho once a day for six days. Then on the seventh day, they marched around it seven times and shouted the seventh time, and the priests blew their trumpets. The walls of the city fell down flat! So the people just walked straight into the city. They killed every person and every animal, because God had told them that everything in the city was devoted* to him. Only Rahab and her family were saved alive. So Jericho was taken without the loss of one single Israelite.

But one man, Achan, stole some money and clothes and hid them in his tent. (See Joshua 7.) (All the money and clothes were supposed to be given to Joshua for God's use.) Then the Israelites attacked a little town called Ai; but thirty-six Israelites were killed and Israel's army was driven off. It was all Achan's fault, for stealing the money and clothes for himself[†2]. God showed Joshua Achan's sin. Then Achan, all his family, animals, and possessions were stoned to death and destroyed. After this sin was removed from Israel, they attacked Ai again and destroyed it.

Israel was supposed to destroy all the peoples of their new land, but they didn't. Some they let live, but they should have asked the Lord first[†3]. Most of the peoples they destroyed.

Then the land was divided up among the tribes. (See map on page 126.) Caleb received the whole city of Hebron for himself, because he was faithful. The Levites (priests) received 48 cities instead of land. Joshua also received a city. (See Joshua 19:49 and 50.) There were six cities of refuge*; people could go to one of them for protection and a fair trial if they committed a crime.

Joshua was old and about ready to die. (See Joshua 23 and 24.) He spoke first to the leaders of Israel. He told them to obey the laws of the Lord. He warned them about worshiping idols and warned them not to marry anyone who was not an Israelite. God would not bless them if they sinned in these ways. He would remove them from their land.

Joshua's final speech was to all Israel. He reminded them of God's miraculous acts: his saving them from Egypt, his protecting them and feeding them in the desert, his fighting for them against their enemies. Joshua warned them to be sure to obey God and follow him. The people renewed the covenant with God and promised to serve him. (See Joshua 24:24.) The book ends with Joshua's death.

LESSONS FROM JOSHUA

[†1] — Who is this "commander of the Lord's army?" (See Joshua 5:13-15.) It is my opinion that he is Christ, appearing in human form many years before his birth as Jesus of Nazareth. He appeared other times, too, in the *Old Testament*. Abraham met him more than once, but he saw him in Genesis 12:7 and 17:1. In Genesis 18 God comes to Abraham as three men! Probably, this is God in three persons—Father, Son, and Spirit. (See especially Genesis 18:22ff, where two of the "men" went down into Sodom, but Abraham remained with God and talked with him. This is like the Father

remaining in heaven when his Son and the Spirit came down to earth.)

Isaac also saw him (Genesis 26:2 and 24) and so did Jacob. (See Genesis 28:10-15 and 35:1 and 9; compare Genesis 48:3.) Some believe Jacob even "wrestled" with him (Genesis 32:22-32).

Moses and the leaders of Israel saw him (Exodus 24:9-11). Then he appeared here to Joshua as "the commander of God's army." He will also appear to others later on in our study. (See Isaiah 6, for example.)

†2 — Achan's sin resulted in the death of several innocent people, including his family. Innocent people always pay for the sins of guilty people. Every innocent baby grows up to sin and die, because of Adam's sin so long ago. Above all, Jesus, the Innocent One, died because of *our* sins.

†3 — God had told Joshua to ask him if Joshua had any questions or didn't know what to do next. The way he could ask God anything was to ask the priest to "cast lots." This would be like when we play dice*. But the *Old Testament* priests used certain dry animal bones. They could read their meaning and tell Joshua what God wanted. (See Proverbs* 16:33.)

JUDGES

SUMMARY OF JUDGES

(Date of events: about 1350-1050 B.C.) In Joshua you learned about Israel invading Canaan. They conquered most of it and divided up the land. But they did not destroy all the enemy nations living in Canaan. In Judges you learn about the leaders who kept fighting these enemies of Israel within Canaan.

The Book of Judges could be summed up by these five words:

1. **Sin**—Some of the Israelites forgot God and worshipped false gods.
2. **Slavery**—An enemy nation would conquer them and make them slaves.
3. **Sorrow**—The people were sorry for their sin and turned to God.
4. **Salvation**—God gave them a judge who would fight and free the Israelites.
5. **Silence**—The people quit turning to God in prayer. (Then it would all start over again, beginning with sin.)

Judges describes a crazy time in Israel's history. When the people worshipped idols, another nation would conquer them. Then the Israelites would be sorry and God would send a ruler (or judge) to save them. Peace would fill the land again.

OUTLINE

1. Israel does not destroy the peoples of the land, so idol worship starts (1:1-3:6)
2. God gives judges to save Israel (3:7-16:31)
3. The Israelites do whatever they want (17-21)

OVERVIEW

The judges were really leaders of Israel. When needed, they fought against Israel's enemies. Another name for a judge would be a ruler or an army general. The judges ruled over only a part of Israel, maybe one or two tribes. Later, a king would rule all Israel. (See I Samuel* 8ff. Remember, "f" means one more chapter or verse; "ff" means a few more chapters or verses. The letters "f" and "ff" stand for "following.")

The Book of Judges is some of the most entertaining reading in the Bible. During the time of the judges, the Israelites just did whatever they felt like doing. "Everyone did as he saw fit." Several parts of the book begin with something like: "The Israelites did evil in the eyes of the Lord." (Judges 22:11, 3:7, 12, 4:1, 6:1, 10:6) When they did evil, then God would let some enemy attack them. (See Judges 3:8, 4:2, 6:1, 10:7, 13:1.) Then they would be sorry for doing evil. So God would give them a judge to fight their enemy, and peace would come to the land.

The main judges of Israel were 1) Othniel, 2) Ehud, 3) Deborah, 4) Gideon, 5) Jephthah, and 6) Samson*. The lesser judges were Shamgar (3:31), Tola (10:1f), Jair (10:3ff), Ibzan, Elon, and Abdon. (See 12:8ff.)

Following are the main judges, the enemies they fought, and a summary of their work:

1. *Othniel* fought against people from northwest Messopotamia and saved Israel from them (Judges 3:7-11).
2. *Ehud* fought Moab, Ammon*, and Amalek*—He lied to the King of Moab, tricked him, and killed him. Then he led Israel's army against the Moabites and destroyed them (Judges 3:12-30).
3. *Deborah* fought Canaan—She was also a prophetess. Barak, another judge, went to the war with Deborah. Barak was afraid, though, at

first. So Deborah got the credit for the victory. Another woman, Jael, killed Sisera, the captain of the Canaanite army. He went to sleep in Jael's tent, so she drove a tent peg through his head. So women got credit instead of Barak. Then Deborah sang a song about her victory (Judges 4:1-5:31).

4. *Gideon* fought Midian*—Midian's army greatly outnumbered Israel's. They conquered northern Israel and occupied the land. The Lord's angel found Gideon in hiding. He told Gideon to stop being afraid and to free Israel from Midian. Gideon asked for proof; "How do I know you are really the Lord?"[t1] The angel did a miracle and then disappeared.[t2] (See Judges 6:17-21.) So Gideon did his first work for God by tearing down an idol's altar![t3] Gideon's next work was that he gathered an army of 32,000 men from the northern tribes. Then he asked God for two more miracles as proof that God really was with him. God did the two miracles (Judges 6:36-40); then he told Gideon that 32,000 men were too many! God finally cut Gideon's army down to 300 men! Now Gideon was afraid again, so God provided one more miracle as proof that Gideon and his army would win (Judges 7:10-15). Just after midnight Gideon and his little army spread out around the Midianites. Gideon and his army blew 300 trumpets, broke 300 big clay jars, held up 300 blazing torches, and shouted. The Midianite army jumped up and began killing each other with their swords! The northern tribes of Israel came out to help finish the job. The Midianite army was totally destroyed. The land had peace for forty years (Judges 6-8).

5. *Jephthah* fought Ammon—Jephthah was a prostitute's son,[t4] but God used him to destroy the Ammonite army and twenty of their towns. But the Israelite tribe of Ephraim* became angry, because Jephthah won the war without their help. So Jephthah also had to fight the Ephraimites. Of the Ephraimites, 42,000 were killed in this "civil war" (Judges 10:6-12:7).

6. *Samson* fought the Philistines*.

His birth (Judges 13)—Unusual things surrounded the birth of Samson. An angel appeared to his parents. He told them that Samson would be a Nazarite. (You can read about the Nazarites in Numbers 6.)

Samson's parents burned a sacrifice to the Lord, and the angel stepped up into the flames and went up to heaven as they watched! So they knew Samson would be special.

*His Marriage** (Judges 14)—God gave Samson great strength. He tore a lion apart with his bare hands. (See Judges 14:5f.) He wanted to marry a Philistine woman.†5 His marriage plans didn't last. But the Lord used it. He gave Samson strength to kill thirty Philistines. And this was just the beginning.

His Revenge (Judges 15)—Samson burned up all the Philistine's crops—grain, olives, and grapevines. So the Philistines burned his "wife" and her father to death. Samson killed many of them then in his anger. In fear of the Philistines, 3,000 Israelites came to Samson. They asked him to turn himself over to them, so the Philistines would not make war against Israel. Samson made the Israelites promise that they wouldn't kill him. Then he let them tie him up with new ropes. When the Philistines saw him all tied up, they shouted and ran up to him. But the Lord gave him strength. He snapped the ropes, took a donkey's jawbone, and beat 1,000 Philistines to death.

His fall (Judges 16)—Samson fell in love with a prostitute named Delilah. He had sex with her and played around with her. He knew he would be strong as long as he kept his Nazarite vow. But she was on the Philistines' side; she kept asking him about his strength. She nagged him so long, he finally told her it came from his Nazarite vow. While he slept, she cut off his hair, and he became like other men. The Philistines took him prisoner, cut out his eyes, and tied him to a mill like a donkey, to grind in prison, blind. But his hair was growing again. One day, the Philistines had a big party. They brought him up to the temple of Dagon, their God, from the prison to make fun of him. But he felt for the main supports of the building, prayed for strength, and God heard him. Samson pushed with all his might. The temple building fell and killed nearly 3,000 Philistines. Samson died with them.

Judges 17-21 tells us about the false religion and evil behavior of the Israelites during the time of the Judges. "There was no king in Israel; everyone did what was right in his own eyes." (See Judges 21-25.)

LESSONS FROM JUDGES

†1 — Gideon kept asking God for miracles, because his faith was so weak. In this case, God was willing to do the miracles, to prove to Gideon that he really was God, and to prove that he was with Gideon. Sometimes God will do this; usually he expects people just to trust him without "proof." Here is a list of the miracles God did for Gideon.

†2 — Miracles:

A. Fire from the rock (Judges 6:11-23)

B. The Lord speaks to Gideon (Judges 6:25f)

C. The dew on the fleece* (Judges 6:36-38)

D. The dew off the fleece (Judges 6:39f)

E. The Lord speaks to Gideon again (Judges 7:4)

F. Gideon overhears his enemy's dream (Judges 7:13-15)

G. Gideon's tiny army destroys Midian (Judges 7:16ff)

†3 — The idols that people used to worship were all sex gods. Baal was the male god, Asherah was the female. The people would worship these gods of fertility and sex by actually having sex before the idols. They would have intercourse in gardens, the shade of oak trees, on high hilltops, because they thought the god would make them fertile there. In fact, nearly the whole ancient world worshipped sex and fertility.

†4 — If Jephthah, a prostitute's son, can be used by God, then it is sure that God can use anyone! God is not concerned about our birth or our background. He already knows all that. He is concerned about our heart—our willingness to believe him and serve him.

Jephthah is mentioned in the roll call of the faithful. (See Hebrews 11:32 in the *New Testament.*) Rahab the prostitute is listed in the same roll call (Hebrews 11:31 as well as James 2:25 in the *New Testament*). She was right with God. Rahab was a foreigner (a Canaanite) and a prostitute, yet *she is in the family tree of Jesus!* (See Matthew 1:5.) It is clear that God will use *anyone* who wants to be used. (See also I Corinthians 1:26-29 in the *New Testament.*)

†5 — All through Samson's life, his problem was an evil desire for women. God used that evil in Samson; how much *more* could he have used Samson if Samson had dealt with his problem? Samson's sin finally blinded, enslaved, and destroyed him.

RUTH

SUMMARY OF RUTH

(Date of events: about 1150-1100 B.C.) In Judges you learned about God's leaders who would fight the enemies of Israel. In Ruth you learn about the private life of poor* people in the time of the judges.

The Book of Ruth is the story of a young Moabite woman who came into the family tree of Jesus Christ. She was the great grandmother of King David*. She had been an idol worshipper. (The Moabites worshipped the sun and other gods.) But she turned to God because of her love for Naomi, her Israelite mother-in-law.

Ruth is a love story. It tells how Ruth the Moabite met and married Boaz. They became great grandparents of King David.

OUTLINE

A. Naomi's husband and sons die (Ruth 1:1-5)

B. Naomi returns from Moab to Israel with Ruth (Ruth 1:6-22)

C. Ruth meets Boaz working in the grain field (Ruth 2)

D. Ruth and Boaz at the grain bin (Ruth 3)

E. Ruth and Boaz get married (Ruth 4:1-17)

F. Ruth is great grandmother of David (Ruth 4:18-22)

OVERVIEW

This sunny little story is about private life during the time of the judges. The Jewish family of Elimelech and Naomi left Israel because there was no food. They moved to Moab and their two sons got married to Moabite women. One of the women was Ruth. The sons died and so did Elimelech. This left Naomi and her two Moabite daughters-in-law. Naomi left for Israel, and Ruth stuck with Naomi. Ruth said, "Where you go, I will go; where you stay, I will stay. Your people will be my people, and your God will be my God." So Ruth stayed with Naomi, even though Ruth was a Moabite. They settled in Bethlehem*.

Because they were poor, Naomi sent Ruth to pick grain in a rich man's field. (This is how God provided for the poor in the *Old Testament.*) The rich man was Boaz. Boaz saw Ruth and liked her immediately. He made sure she got extra grain. Naomi was surprised at how much grain Ruth brought home! So Naomi told Ruth that night, "Get cleaned up and go out to where Boaz is working. When he goes to sleep, go up quietly and cover yourself with his blanket. He is related to us[†1] as a kinsman redeemer*, so he will take care of you." Ruth did as she was told. During the night, Boaz woke up, and there was Ruth at his feet! He decided he wanted to redeem* her if he could, but he was second in line in the family.

The next day Boaz talked the other kinsman redeemer out of redeeming Ruth. Boaz wanted her for himself. So he made a deal with the other man to get Ruth and to get Elimelech's property. The elders of Israel witnessed the deal. Then Naomi was excited and happy, because Boaz married Ruth. Ruth soon had a baby. Naomi was baby-sitter for little Obed*. Later, Obed was the father of Jesse, and Jesse became the father of David.

LESSONS FROM RUTH

†1 — The kinsman redeemer idea is an interesting picture of what Jesus is for us in the *New Testament*. Just as Boaz was related to Ruth, so Jesus is related to us as our Big Brother. (Since we have received the Spirit of sonship and become heirs with Jesus, he is our Big Brother. See Romans 8:15-17 in the *New Testament*.) Just as Boaz redeemed (bought) Ruth to give her a better life, so Jesus has redeemed us to give us not only a better life, but a longer life also. (See Titus 2:11-14 and John 5:24 in the *New Testament*.)

his life, Saul had become so far from God that he even went to a witch to try to find out his future. (See I Samuel 28.) So the first king of Israel died a failure. But David the warrior king took over in his place.

After he cried over the death of Saul and Jonathan (II Samuel 1:19-27), David became king over Judah in Hebron. David's army wiped out all of Saul's army. Then David was made king over all the tribes of Israel. (See II Samuel 5:15.)

David conquered Jerusalem and moved there. He brought the covenant box to Jerusalem also. The Lord was with David in all he did. He made a great promise to David—that a son of his would always rule over God's people.[t1] (See II Samuel 7:16.) Every war David was in, he won, because God was on his side. In all this, David remained humble.

But then David sinned. He had sex with Bathsheba, a married woman. When she became pregnant, David had her husband killed. The Lord confronted David through Nathan the prophet. David was sorry for his sin, and the Lord forgave him. But it was too late. Sin always has bad results. David's life was changed from that time on. The baby born to Bathsheba died, and the people in David's family rebelled, raped, and killed each other. David's son Absalom even set himself up as king in Hebron against David; David had to run away from Jerusalem so he wouldn't be killed. Then Absalom himself was killed by David's army captain, Joab. There was even rebellion within his own army's ranks. David's heart was broken by all this. II Samuel ended with other judgments on David for other sins. David was now an old man. In spite of his sins, he was one of the greatest kings in Israel's history.

LESSONS FROM I AND II SAMUEL

[t1] — In Genesis 12:1-3 God promised Abraham that he would bless all the world through Abraham's family. God renewed that promise to Isaac, Jacob, and Moses. In II Samuel 7:16 he renewed it to David. The promise in II Samuel 7:16 is that a king from David's family will rule forever. That king is Jesus Christ. (See Matthew 1:1, 12:23; John 7:42; Romans 1:3; and Revelation 22:16.)

I AND II KINGS
(Originally One Book)

SUMMARY OF I AND II KINGS

(Date of events: about 970 to 570 B.C.) In I and II Samuel you learned about Samuel the prophet and the first two kings of Israel, Saul and David. In I and II Kings we learn about the rest of the kings and the end of the kingdoms.

Solomon* is the last king of all Israel; the rest are kings either of southern Israel or northern Israel. After Solomon, the united kingdom split in two; the northern tribes were united under their first king, Jeroboam. They are called either "Israel" or "Ephraim." The southern tribes were united around the temple of Solomon in Jerusalem. They were called Judah. I and II Kings begins with the death of King David and ends with all of Israel being punished for their sins. God used Assyria* to conquer the northern kingdom in 722 B.C. Assyria took the people of Israel into captivity as slaves. Later, God used Babylon* to conquer Judah and take them into captivity as slaves in 586 B.C.*

The aim of Kings is to look at each king to see if he obeyed God and kept the law of Moses.

OUTLINE

A. King Solomon's reign (I Kings 1:1-12:24)

B. Kings of the North and South (I Kings 12:25-16:34)

C. Prophets: Elijah and Elisha (I Kings 17-II Kings 13)

D. Eleven kings and the exile* of Israel (II Kings 14-17)

E. Eight kings and the exile of Judah (II Kings 18-25)

OVERVIEW

I and II Kings were originally one book about the rest of the kings of Israel. Before David's death, Adonijah, one of his sons, set himself up as king. But David quickly made Solomon king, and Solomon had Adonijah killed. Solomon took over the kingdom. Then the Lord spoke to him in a dream: "Ask whatever you want, and I will give it to you." (See I Kings 3:5.) Solomon could have asked for wealth or glory or fame; instead, he asked for wisdom to lead God's people. God gave him wisdom, but he gave him wealth and glory and fame, too.

Solomon built a glorious temple for God, so God no longer lived in a tent (the tabernacle). The Temple in Jerusalem was then the richest building in the world. It lasted 400 years, up to the time Babylon destroyed Jerusalem (about 586 B.C.). All sacrifices were offered at the temple. The Ark of the Covenant* (covenant box) was there, too. Solomon knew even the highest heavens could not contain God, but God did come to the temple and live there, too.

Solomon was the greatest, wisest king ever. He built fleets of ships; he did scientific investigation and study; he wrote books of proverbs and songs; his wisdom and wealth were known all over the world. Solomon did a very foolish thing: he married 700 wives! They were from other countries, and Solomon began to worship their false gods. More about Solomon is in II Chronicles 1-9.

Solomon's son Rehoboam was a fool. He was the next king. He listened to his young friends instead of the older men, and he split the kingdom of Israel (I Kings 12). Jeroboam ruled over the northern tribes (Israel), and Rehoboam over the southern (Judah). The southern kingdom was three tribes: Judah, Benjamin and Simeon, but all were called Judah. Jeroboam built idols for Israel to worship. The Lord punished him, and he died. (Read I Kings 4:1-18.)

There were eighteen more kings of Judah and one "queen" (Athaliah) after Rehoboam. They ruled from about 915 B.C. to 586 B.C. (It was in 586 B.C. that Babylon came and destroyed Jerusalem.) Some of the kings were good men, but most were weak and evil. The southern kingdom was slowly losing its strength. Hezekiah* was the last good *and* great king (about 715-685 B.C.); Josiah was the last good king (about 640-610 B.C.).

Here is a list of Judah's nineteen rulers after Rehoboam:

Kings	Reign	Importance	Good or Bad
1. Abijah	3 years	Fought against northern kingdom and won (vs. Jeroboam)	Mainly bad
2. Asa	41 years	Made treaty with Aram*	Mainly bad
3. Jehoshaphat	25 years	Destroyed idol worship. Conquered Judah's enemies	Good
4. Jehoram	7 years	War; died of terrible bowel disease (See II Chronicles 21)	Bad
5. Ahaziah	1 year	Not important; executed	Bad
6. Athaliah	7 years	Queen-mother of Ahaziah. Executed by Levites	Bad
7. Joash	40 years	Repaired God's temple then rejected God	Good then bad
8. Amaziah	29 years	Defeated Seir in war then set up false gods	Good then bad
9. Uzziah	16 years	Much building. Defeated enemies. Died of leprosy.	Good (but sinned; see II Chronicles 26:16-21)
10. Jotham	16 years	Built towns; conquered the Ammonites	Good
11. Ahaz	16 years	Closed the Lord's temple, set up idol-worship; lost in war.	Bad
12. Hezekiah	29 years	Reopened the temple with Isaiah's help; God conquered a great invader (See Isaiah 36 and 37)	Good

13. Manasseh	55 years	Set up idol-worship all over Judah—even *in* the temple. Then removed them.	Bad then good
14. Amon	2 years	Set up idol-worship; he was killed by his own men.	Bad
15. Josiah	31 years	God's law was found during his rule. He removed idol-worship. Died in battle.	Good
16. Jehoahaz	3 months	Taken by Pharaoh Neco to Egypt where he died.	Bad
17. Jehoiakim	11 years	Originally called Eliakim. Paid protection money to Pharaoh Neco. Finally conquered by Nebuchadnezzar*, king of Babylon	Bad
18. Jehoiachin	3 months	Surrendered to Nebuchadnezzar and died in Babylon.	Bad
19. Zedekiah	11 years	Originally called Mattaniah. Weak king who finally was led away blind to Babylon.	Bad[†1]

The story of the end of Israel is contained in II Kings 17; II Kings 25 contains the story of the end of Judah. Judah and Jerusalem were destroyed by Babylon.

Before leaving the books of Kings, it is good to mention two great prophets of Israel—Elijah and Elisha. Elijah's story is in I Kings 17 through II Kings 2; Elisha's story begins in I Kings 19:16. He took over from Elijah in II Kings 2. His story ends in II Kings 13. Their job was to call the people of the northern kingdom back to worship God again. Elijah and Elisha disagreed with the kings in Israel. The kings of Israel had rejected the Lord; it was necessary that God send someone to lead them right. Elijah and Elisha were those leaders.

Both of these prophets were strange men. Their stories are very interesting reading. They did many miracles for God. They called the people again and again to repent* and to follow God. If you start reading their stories, you will find it hard to stop! (Read I Kings 17-II Kings 13.)

LESSONG FROM I AND II KINGS

†1 — As I read the list of kings, I am reminded that in a few years I will be just as dead as they are. So will you. It is so important for us to leave behind a memory of good, not evil. So obey God—treat all people with love and respect.

I and II CHRONICLES
(Originally One Book)

SUMMARY OF I AND II CHRONICLES

(Date of events: from the beginning of humanity [Adam] to King Cyrus* of Persia—about 530 B.C.) In I and II Kings you learned about the kings of Israel, beginning with Solomon. Then the kingdom divided and the rest of the books are about the kings of both the northern and southern kingdoms. Both kingdoms were destroyed. Now, in Chronicles, you learn about all Bible history, up to the rebuilding of Jerusalem and God's temple. Chronicles ends with the Jews leaving Babylon (the Persian Empire) and rebuilding Jerusalem.

OUTLINE

A. Tracing the Jews' family lines (I Chronicles 1-9)

B. King David and getting ready to build the temple (I Chronicles 10-29)

C. King Solomon and the Temple of God (II Chronicles 1-9)

D. The split kingdoms, the kings of Judah, the exile, and the return to Jerusalem (II Chronicles 10-36)

OVERVIEW

Chronicles means *a record of events*. Chronicles summarizes all the history of the Jews, so the books cover thousands of years. Ezra the priest may be the main writer. He answers the questions, "Is God still with us?" and "Does God still have plans for us?" Answer: Yes!

The books of Chronicles are a history of God's work with people. The books are like a series of sermons on God's past choices among Israel for his people. The kings and the temple are not enough to make God's people secure. It is only *God* who makes his people secure! If his people believe and obey his words, they will have success. (See II Chronicles 7:14 and 20:20.) Chronicles renews Israel's hope for the coming of Jesus Christ, by remembering the "good old days" of their past great kings. Chronicles sums up all the books we have already studied, but it stresses the importance of the temple and God's promise to David. (See I Chronicles 17.) Even though Jerusalem and God's temple were destroyed, even though God's people became slaves in foreign lands, there is hope for the future. One day the Messiah, Jesus Christ, will come. He will rule on David's throne *forever*.

EZRA

SUMMARY OF EZRA

(Date of events: about 458-445 B.C.) Chronicles describes the history of God's people. They seldom obeyed, but often disobeyed God. Finally, he punished them by sending them to other nations, including Assyria, then Babylon, as slaves. In Ezra (and Nehemiah) you learn about the return of God's people to Jerusalem and the rebuilding of the temple and the city.

Ezra was a priest and a scribe*. His story and Nehemiah's were originally in the same book. Ezra is a book about the return of the Jews from Babylon and the rebuilding of the temple of the Lord. Cyrus the Persian was the king of Babylon who let them return.

OUTLINE

A. The Jews return from Babylon to build the temple (Ezra 1-6)

B. Ezra returns from Babylon and helps change the Jews for the better (Ezra 7-10)

OVERVIEW

Much of Ezra is boring to read because of all his lists. He listed the numbers and names of the temple dishes, the people, the animals, and the leaders who returned to Jerusalem. He even listed those who married foreign wives! He records the official letters written back and forth to the emperors. These emperors gave permission to Ezra and Nehemiah to rebuild the temple and the city walls. The enemies of the Jews did not want Jerusalem to be rebuilt. But the Jews went right on building, because they had three emperors' permission to build. (King Cyrus, King Xerxes*, and King Artaxerxes*, all Persians, gave permission.) Ezra could be called the "Father of Modern Judaism." He made the people obey the law. He even forced those who had married foreign wives to get a divorce. He was a committed servant of God, careful to obey all God had commanded. The people gladly obeyed Ezra, and God blessed those who confessed their sins and obeyed. So Jerusalem's temple was rebuilt and worship began again.

NEHEMIAH

SUMMARY OF NEHEMIAH

(Date of events: about 445-430 B.C.) In Ezra you learned about the Jews' return from Babylon, rebuilding the temple, and beginning the worship of God again. In Nehemiah you learn about Nehemiah returning from Babylon and rebuilding the city wall, so the people in Jerusalem would be protected.

Nehemiah was originally in the same book as Ezra. His story takes place just after the events in Ezra. His job was to rebuild Jerusalem's walls. This protected the city and the temple from enemies around them.

OUTLINE

A. Nehemiah's first return from Babylon (Nehemiah 1:1-2:10)

B. Nehemiah's rebuilds the walls (Nehemiah 2:11-12:47)

C. Nehemiah's second return from Babylon and the changes he made (Nehemiah 13)

OVERVIEW

Nehemiah is a great story of leadership. It began with Nehemiah serving King Artaxerxes in Persia. Nehemiah was sad about Jerusalem being in ruins. The king noticed how sad he was. So he allowed Nehemiah to return to Jerusalem. By night, Nehemiah saw that

Jerusalem's walls were broken down and the gates were burned. He felt that he just *had* to rebuild the walls, so he got others to help. The people worked hard, even though their enemies tried to stop them. First the enemies made fun of them. When the Jews kept building, the enemies threatened them. So the builders worked with their weapons ready at hand. Then the enemies sent false prophets to tell the Jews to stop, but Nehemiah prayed that God would help him. So the walls were done in only fifty-two days! (See Nehemiah 6:15.) Then Ezra the scribe brought out the law and read it to the Jews. The people all cried as they heard the scriptures. They worshipped God, and a great revival began to spread. The new walls of Jerusalem were dedicated to the Lord. Then Nehemiah cleared out the temple and made the people do right. He even beat up some of the men and pulled out their hair! (See Nehemiah 13:25.) Nehemiah really meant business![1]

LESSONS FROM NEHEMIAH

[1] — Nehemiah was a man who just kept doing what God wanted. He refused to give up. If you know that God has given you something to do, **do it**, and never give up. God will bless those who keep on doing what they know is right.

ESTHER

SUMMARY OF ESTHER

(Date of events: about 475-470 B.C.) In Nehemiah you learned about Nehemiah's work to build the walls around Jerusalem. In Esther you learn about a beautiful Jewish girl who saved the Jewish people from death in the Persian Empire.

Esther was a Jewish slave in the Persian Empire. King Xerxes chose her to be queen because of her beauty. She risked her life to save all her own people from death during her rule as queen.

OUTLINE

A. King Xerxes chooses Esther as his new queen. (Esther 1-2)

B. Evil Haman tries to have all the Jews killed (Esther 3-5)

C. Haman dies by hanging (Esther 6-7)

D. The Jews defeat their enemies (Esther 8-10)

OVERVIEW

(Esther 1-2) King Xerxes had a party. All his men friends were there. His wife, Queen Vashti, had a party for all her women friends, too. The king got a little drunk; he sent for his wife so he could show all the men how beautiful she was. But she said, "No. I won't come to your party." The king was very angry. He divorced her and began looking for an even more beautiful girl to be his queen. He liked Esther best of all and chose her as his queen.

During this time, Esther's uncle, Mordecai, who had raised her as his adopted daughter, told Esther that King Xerxes' life was in danger. Two soldiers planned to kill the king. Esther warned Xerxes, and the soldiers were executed by hanging. So Mordecai had saved King Xerxes' life.

(Esther 3) King Xerxes appointed a rich evil man named Haman to a high place in the kingdom; Haman became "Prime Minister." All the people bowed their heads before Haman—except for Mordecai. He refused to bow, so Haman was angry. He wanted to kill Mordecai, but not only Mordecai; he wanted to kill *all* the Jews. Haman gave King Xerxes 375 tons of silver to get the king on his side. So the king made a new law that all the Jews—men, women, and children—should be killed. Xerxes didn't know Queen Esther was Jewish. Once a law was made in Persia, it could *never* be changed.

(Esther 4) Mordecai told Queen Esther what Haman had gotten the king to do. He wanted Esther to ask King Xerxes to please change the law. Jews were to be killed all over the empire on a certain day. Esther knew that if anyone went to the king without being invited, that uninvited person would be killed. So she asked all Jews everywhere to go without food for three days. She wanted them to pray for her, because she knew she had to go see the king without being invited. She decided to fast* and pray, too.

(Esther 5) Esther was so beautiful! When she went uninvited to the king, he saw her and invited her in. So Esther asked the king and evil Haman to come to a party two days in a row. During these two days, Haman had his servants build a huge gallows*, 75 feet tall. He planned to kill Mordecai on the gallows.

(Esther 6) That night King Xerxes couldn't sleep. He had a slave read the record of his rule to him. The slave read the part about Mordecai saving the king's life. (See Esther 2:19-23.) The king had never thanked Mordecai for saving his life. So he asked Haman, "How would you publicly thank a man you wanted to thank?" Haman thought the king wanted to thank him, so he said, "Dress him up in one of your royal robes. Have him ride one of your royal horses. Have a high person in the kingdom lead the horse and yell, 'Look how the king thanks a man he wants to thank!'" So King Xerxes had Haman do all that for Mordecai! Haman was really embarrassed.

(Esther 7) After Haman led Mordecai's horse around the city, he had to hurry to get to Esther's party on time the second day. The king was so happy with Esther, he promised her anything she wanted. So Esther said, "Your Majesty, Haman is trying to kill me and all the other Jews!" The king was so angry that he had Haman hanged on his own seventy-five-foot gallows!

(Esther 8) Since King Xerxes could not change his first law to kill all Jews, he made a second law. The second law said that the Jews could fight anyone who tried to kill them.

(Esther 9) So the Jews destroyed all those who tried to kill them until they had no enemies left to fight.

(Esther 10) Mordecai had this story written down. To this day, the Jews have a party every year in February or March to remember Esther and the Jews being saved. It is called the *Feast of Purim**. The book of Esther ends with King Xerxes promoting Mordecai to second in power in the Persian Empire. So God blessed and protected the Jews even in a foreign land.

Now we've come to the second part of the *Old Testament*. The first part was history. The second part is wise writings or Wisdom Literature.

JOB

SUMMARY OF JOB

(Date of events: about 2,000 B.C.; date of writing: maybe 1,000 B.C.)
In Esther you learned about a beautiful Jewish girl who became queen
of Persia. She saved her people from certain death. In Job, you learn
how Job* kept his faith in God, even though he suffered terribly.

Job was a good man, but God allowed Satan to attack him anyway.
Job kept his faith in God, even though he lost his children, his wealth,
and his health. Even his friends were of no help to him; they thought
he must have been a terrible sinner to suffer so much. But in the end,
God rewarded Job's faith.

OUTLINE

A. The "wager" between God and Satan (or Satan makes a bet with
   God) (Job 1-2)

B. Job and his three friends argue (Job 3-31)

C. Elihu speaks (Job 32-37)

D. The Lord speaks (Job 38-42:6)

E. The Lord rewards Job (Job 42:7-17)

OVERVIEW

(Job 1-3) Job was a good man who was very rich. Every day Job offered sacrifices to God and prayed for his children. He was like a priest for his family. But in heaven, God and Satan talked about Job.[†1] Satan told God, "Of course Job worships you! Look how rich and famous you've made him! If you take all that away from him, he'll *hate* you!" So God gave Satan permission to take away Job's wealth and fame. In anger, Satan destroyed Job's wealth, and killed his children. But Job still trusted and worshiped God. Again, Satan spoke to God: "Take away Job's health and he'll hate you!" So God let him. Satan gave Job a terrible, painful disease all over his body. The disease became so bad that Job had awful sores; his skin became infected with boils; pus was all over him. He even had maggots on him. (See Job 7:5.) He was so sad and hurting so badly that he couldn't sleep. Even the thought of food made him sick. He was miserable, but he still trusted and worshipped God.

(Job 4-31) Then Job's three friends came. They were so shocked at the way Job looked that they couldn't speak for a whole week. When they did speak, they all accused him of sin. They said, "You must have done something awful, or you wouldn't be suffering like this! You should repent, Job. Suffering is always the result of sin." They weren't much comfort, were they?[†2] All Job could do was defend himself over and over. He knew that he was not an evil person. He wished God would rescue him and defend him.

(Job 32-37) When Job finally stopped defending himself, another friend, younger than the other three, spoke up. Elihu said, "Job, you shouldn't defend yourself; you should defend God instead. Only God is really righteous." Elihu was right, of course, but this wasn't much help to poor Job.

(Job 38:1-42:6) When Elihu stopped talking, Job said nothing. God came to them then, in a storm. Instead of taking Job's side, God just asked Job a lot of questions. With all his questions, he showed Job several things:

- Job didn't understand how the world was created.

- Job didn't understand nature—heat, cold, wind, rain, snow, hail, oceans, etc.
- Job didn't understand animals—how they mate, how they live, how to tame them, etc.
- Job didn't understand how God rules the world. So Job couldn't understand suffering, either.

(Job 42:7-17) Job was sorry he had spoken about God as he had. Now that he had seen God, he said, "I repent!"

Then God told Job's three friends that they were wrong and Job was right. God said that Job would pray for them, and God would forgive them. Then God blessed Job again; he gave Job even more wealth and fame than before. He became so famous that even you and I know about him!

LESSONS FROM JOB

†1 — Job did not know about Satan. He only knew that he trusted and worshipped God, no matter what! We need to be like Job. If bad things happen to us, we must still trust God. If we suffer our whole life long, we will still have an eternity of joy in the next life if we keep our trust and faith in God. (If you are a good reader, I recommend that you read *Disappointment with God*, by Phillip Yancey [Zondervan] if you are interested in faith and suffering.)

†2 — Some people today teach that we suffer only if we sin. God says this is a false teaching. Suffering and death are just a part of life. We should trust God anyway. One day he'll make everything right. (See Romans 8:28, James 1:2ff, esp. verse 12, and Romans 5:1-5 in the *New Testament*.) Of course, Jesus suffered, and we know he did not sin. He suffered for *our* sins.

PSALMS

SUMMARY OF PSALMS

(Date of writing: about 1500-400 B.C.) In Job you learned about a man who kept trusting God, even though he suffered. In Psalms we learn about worship in Israel a long time ago.

Psalms is a book of songs, poems, and prayers. They were used by people in Israel to worship God or as prayers to God.

OUTLINE

(The Psalms can't really be outlined. But they are divided into five different books.)

Book 1: Psalms 1-41
Book 2: Psalms 42-72
Book 3: Psalms 73-89
Book 4: Psalms 90-106
Book 5: Psalms 107-150

OVERVIEW

Many of the psalms were written by David. His name is in the title of seventy-three of them. Other people wrote some psalms, too, or used the psalms in worship. Titles are in front of some psalms. These titles may tell us several things:

A. Who wrote the psalm (See Psalm 3's title.)

B. What the name of the group of psalms is (See the titles of Psalms 120-134.)

C. What kind of psalm it is (See Psalm 32's title or Psalm 16's title.)

D. What kind of music or instrument was played with the psalm (See Psalm 22's title or Psalm 8's title.)

E. What kind of worship the psalm was used for (See Psalm 100's title.)

F. What was happening when the psalm was written (See Psalm 51's title.)

Thirty-four of the psalms have no title at all. All the psalms are a kind of poetry, but they don't rhyme. Their poetry is like the Proverbs' poetry—it is a poetry of ideas. Some ideas contrast; some ideas complete a thought; some ideas build together one main thought. The good thing about this kind of poetry is that it can be translated from one language to another. Rhyme would be impossible to translate!

Psalms may be the most important book in the whole *Old Testament.* It has more prophecies about Jesus in it than any other book. When the *New Testament* quotes the *Old Testament,* nearly half of the quotes come from the Psalms. So the Book of Psalms tells us more about Jesus than any other *Old Testament* book.

You can read the Psalms to learn how to live right. (See Psalm 1.) You can read them to find out about Jesus. (See Psalms 2, 22, 110 and others.) You can read them to worship God, or to pray (See Psalm 19:7-14.) or even to learn some about history. (See Psalm 107, for example.) But the best way to read the Psalms is in worship. (Read Psalm 139, for example.)

The Psalms were written by people who needed a person to relate to. The law, written on stone tablets, was too hard and impersonal. The Psalms are from wise people who wanted to know God personally. (Read some verses of Psalm 119, for example.) In trying to live the law, people became angry at themselves or frustrated. But when they thought about God, they were filled with thanksgiving and praise. They wanted to know God, not just the law. So they wrote the psalms out of their life and dreams and hopes. The Psalms are some of the best reading in the whole Bible. They are by people who know God and his forgiveness.

I love to read the Psalms for my personal devotions*. Many *New Testaments* include Psalms, because people love them. There is nothing quite like them in the *New Testament.* Believers in Jesus have used them in worship and praise since the church began nearly 2,000 years ago. There is so much variety in the Psalms that you will probably never get tired of them. My personal favorite psalms are 1, 2, 8, 15, 16, 19, 22, 23, 24, 31, 32, 37, 42, 45, 46, 51, 84, 100, 102, 103, 104, 110, 119, and 139. As you read the Psalms in your Bible, these and many others may speak to your heart. Enjoy the Psalms!

PROVERBS

SUMMARY OF PROVERBS

(Date of writing: about 1,000-700 B.C.) In Psalms you learned about Israel's worship. In Proverbs you learn how to live a good life.

Proverbs is a book of short, smart sayings. Proverbs helps us be happy and keep out of trouble. Wise men, especially King Solomon, wrote the Proverbs. They wrote to teach us how to see as God sees, so our lives will be good. If we can live by the Proverbs, God will be pleased with our lives.

OUTLINE

(Proverbs really can't be outlined. It is like a string of pearls.)

A. Why Solomon wrote Proverbs (Proverbs 1:1-7)

B. Solomon's proverbs, teaching: (Proverbs 1:8-29:27)

    1. How young people can stay out of trouble;

    2. How young people can enjoy long, healthy, happy lives;

    3. How wise people can become even wiser.

C. Proverbs of Agur (Proverbs 30)

D. Proverbs of King Lemuel (Proverbs 31:1-9)

E. The perfect wife (Proverbs 31:10-31)

OVERVIEW

Proverbs is for all people in all nations.[†1] After 1:1, the word *Israel* does not appear in Proverbs. Instead, the word "man" (meaning "people") is used over 100 times. This means that Proverbs is for everyone, not just one nation. Also, every nation has its own "proverbs."

A proverb is a very short, very wise saying, Usually it will have only ten to fifteen words in it, but it means a lot. I can read a proverb once, and it has one meaning. Later, I'll read it again, and it means something else to me. Solomon was the wisest man who ever lived, and he knew how to put a lot of meaning into a short sentence!

We even have proverbs in our country. Maybe you will know some of these proverbs: a) "The early bird gets the worm." That may mean that if you get up early you'll get more done. b) "You catch more flies with honey than with vinegar." That may mean you'll have more friends if you're sweet to them and not sour. c) We even have some that contradict each other, like: "A rolling stone gathers no moss." But "A wandering bee gets the honey." The first one means you should stay in one place, but the second one means you shouldn't. Well, the *Old Testament* Proverbs are like that, too. (See Proverbs 26:4-5, for example.)

LESSONS FROM PROVERBS

†1 — The Book of Proverbs was given to us by God to teach young people. Parents should teach their sons and daughters from proverbs. My wife and I tried to use the Proverbs to teach our children: a) right from wrong, b) how to be self-disciplined; c) how to obey authority, d) how to stay away from bad people, bad behavior, and bad talk; e) how to learn from older, wiser good people, f) and most important how to fear the Lord, to respect and honor, obey and love Him. (See Proverbs 1:7 and 9:10.) If children can learn these things from Proverbs, they will be happy and healthy, and they'll live a life pleasing to God and other people. My favorite proverbs are 3:5-8, 17:22, and 20:2-9, but there are many other good ones.

ECCLESIASTES

SUMMARY OF ECCLESIASTES

(Date of writing: about 975 B.C.) In Proverbs you learned how to live a good life. In Ecclesiastes you learn how empty life is without God.

Solomon probably wrote Ecclesiastes toward the end of his life. He describes his search for meaning. He had begun with God, but he began to fall away from God when he married wives who worshipped idols. He tried to please his wives instead of God. So he searched for life's meaning apart from God. In the end, he had to admit that the meaning of life is to be found in obeying God.

OUTLINE

A. Life is boring and meaningless (Ecclesiastes 1:1-11)

B. The search for meaning (Ecclesiastes 1:12-12:7)

C. The meaning of life: trust and obey God (Ecclesiastes 12:8-14)

OVERVIEW

Ecclesiastes says that life on earth is without meaning. Life is boring and repeats the same things over and over. Solomon says that even wisdom is meaningless, because it brings sadness. As a dog* dies, so does a lion; as a slave dies, so does the king. Man dies like the animals. Death is the most meaningless of all, because God has put eternity in people's hearts. (See Ecclesiastes 3:11.) We all want to live forever and to learn everything about the universe. But we can never do it, because we die. Solomon seemed to be depressed and frustrated in his search for meaning in this life, especially when he thought about his own death. He says we can enjoy our food, our drink, our work, and our wife or husband. These things don't give us any lasting meaning, but we can still enjoy them. (See Ecclesiastes 2:24 and 9:9.) But the key word of Ecclesiastes is "meaningless." It is used about forty times, because even the wisest of men could not find lasting meaning in this earthly life.

Ecclesiastes ends with a symbolic look at death. (See Ecclesiastes 12:1-8.) But the book really ends with this conclusion: "Fear God and obey him, for this is all a man is!" So the meaning of life can be found only in our personal relationship with God, through Jesus Christ. (See Ecclesiastes 12:13 and John 14:6 in the *New Testament.*)

SONG OF SONGS

SUMMARY OF SONG OF SONGS

(Date of writing: about 950 B.C.) In Ecclesiastes you learned that life is meaningless without God. In Song of Songs you learn about the love between a husband and wife.

Song of Songs was written about Solomon. He had 700 wives and 300 slave wives (concubines). If anyone knew women, it was Solomon! Song of Songs means it is the greatest of all songs. It is a very symbolic song about love and marriage. It is the only book of its kind in the Bible.

OUTLINE

A. The lovers' first meeting (Song of Songs 1:1-2:7)

B. The lovers' second meeting (Song of Songs 2:8-3:5)

C. The lovers' third meeting (Song of Songs 3:6-5:1)

D. The lovers' fourth meeting (Song of Songs 5:2-6:3)

E. The lovers' fifth meeting (Song of Songs 6:4-8:4)

F. The lovers' sixth meeting (Song of Songs 8:5-14)

OVERVIEW

Song of Songs is about sexual love in marriage. The Jews were not allowed to read it unless they were at least thirty years old or married. It is beautiful poetry. It may have been used as a drama or a play. It begins with the girl wanting to be kissed; it ends with her asking her husband to make love to her. Clearly, God wants all sexual love to be in marriage *only*. Sexual relationships are never for unmarried people.[†1] The worldly way of sex is not right; it has been sick and evil since the sin of Adam. But God wants us to enjoy sex *in marriage*. Whatever is accepted by both the wife and the husband is okay in marriage.[†2] God's rules for sexual happiness are clear: a) no sex before marriage; b) sex in marriage only; c) no sex outside the marriage, once a couple are married.

LESSONS FROM SONG OF SONGS

[†1] — Herbert J. Miles is a Christian medical doctor. I recommend his book *Sexual Understanding Before Marriage* (Zondervan) for people who are not married. The hardest part of Christian sex is controlling our thoughts. Before I was a Christian, I was addicted to all kinds of pornography. When I became a Christian, that was my hardest struggle. God patiently worked with me and helped me overcome my sexual problems over the years. The key is: control your thoughts. (See Romans 8:5-8 in the *New Testament*.) Sexual fantasy is sinful; it is not good for you. In fact, pornography often leads to rape or other sexual evils and sinful behavior. If you have a problem with sex, remember this: with God's help, prayer, and Bible study, you can overcome it. When you look at pornography, a special chemical is released in your brain. It is the same chemical that makes us never forget a car accident or other terrible experience. Feed your mind God's word, not evil thoughts. That is the only way to overcome this problem. (See Romans 12:1 and 2 in the *New Testament*.)

[†2] — I recommend for married couples to read a book by Herbert J. Miles, a Christian medical doctor. It is entitled *Sexual Happiness in Marriage* (Zondervan). This book is for married people *only*!

Now we've come to the third part of the *Old Testament*. The first part was history. The second part was Wisdom Literature. The third part is Prophets.

ISAIAH

SUMMARY OF ISAIAH

(Date of events: about 740-680 B.C.) In Song of Songs you learned about the love between a husband and wife. In Isaiah you learn about Isaiah, the prophet of Jerusalem, and the future of that part of the world.

Isaiah was the greatest of the writing prophets. He wrote the longest book. He saw Jesus Christ more clearly than any other prophet. (See Isaiah 53.) More than 100 years before it happened, he predicted the fall and destruction of Jerusalem. He predicted accurately the Babylonian invasion of Jerusalem, the seventy-year exile in Babylon, and the Jews' return to Jerusalem.

OUTLINE

A. Messages about Jerusalem and Judah (Isaiah 1-12)

B. Messages about other nations (Isaiah 13-23)

C. Worldwide judgment by God (Isaiah 24-35)

D. Assyria now, Babylon later (Isaiah 36-39)

E. The Lord of history (Isaiah 40-48)

F. Future salvation and the Servant of the Lord (Isaiah 49-61)

G. Eternal glory and judgment (Isaiah 62-66)

OVERVIEW

Next to Psalms, Isaiah is my favorite *Old Testament* book. Although he lived long before Jesus was born, Jesus appeared to him! (See Isaiah 6:1-10 and John 12:39-41 in the *New Testament*.) When Isaiah saw Jesus, his life was forever changed. People don't see very often into the spirit world or into heaven, but Isaiah saw Jesus Christ ruling on his throne in heaven! (Isaiah 6.) He heard the seraphs* shout "Holy, Holy, Holy." From that day on, Isaiah called God "the Holy One of Israel." He does this 26 times in his book, beginning in Isaiah 1:4.

(Isaiah 1-12) Isaiah talks about how bad the people of Jerusalem are[†1]. They worship God in the temple using all the right prayers and all the right forms, but they do evil all week long. But God promises to purify others anyway, in the future. (See Isaiah 4:3 and 4; also see Isaiah 11:1-5.) But first God will not protect them for a time, and they will be punished. (See Isaiah 5:5 and 6.) He will use another country (Babylon) to punish Jerusalem. Then God will send his son to help them and to save all nations forever. (See Isaiah 9, especially verses 6 and 7; also see 11:10, 12, and 16.) Isaiah sings praises to God for what God has done and will yet do. (See Isaiah 12.)

(Isaiah 13-23) Even though God will use Assyria and Babylon to punish his people, he will also punish Assyria and Babylon for their pride. He will also punish the other nations of the world for their sins. God really did use Babylon as "the rod of his anger" to "spank" the nations. Then he also destroyed Babylon.

(Isaiah 24-35) Isaiah listed many other countries God will punish. Much of this part of Isaiah is very negative reading. But in the middle of all this negative stuff are "flashes of light." Take Isaiah 25, for instance. In verses 6-9 Isaiah says that God will have a great party for all nations. At this party God will destroy death forever, and people will never cry or suffer again. No matter what happens in this world *God's people will win!*[†2] (See also Isaiah 30:20 and 21.)

In Isaiah 36-39, two things are recorded for us: a) Isaiah 36 and 37 records Assyria's great army attacking Jerusalem. They surrounded Jerusalem's walls and made fun of God. They said God couldn't save Jerusalem. No other gods saved any other city. They said, "What makes you think your God is any stronger than the other idols?" King

Hezekiah and Isaiah the prophet prayed together about the Assyrian army, and God answered their prayer. That very night, the Angel of the Lord killed 185,000 Assyrian soldiers. So Sennacherib*, the king of Assyria, went back home. There, he was killed by his own sons.†3

b) In Isaiah 38 and 39 Hezekiah almost died of a sickness. God did a miracle and gave him fifteen more years to live. Stupidly, Hezekiah showed some Babylonian men his treasury of gold and silver. After the men left, Isaiah told him that in the future, Babylon would conquer Jerusalem and take all the treasure away. But Hezekiah wasn't worried. He knew this would happen in the future, after he had died.

(Isaiah 40-48) Isaiah spoke for God. He predicted the Jews' exile in Babylon and the return from the exile. He even predicted the name of the King of Persia who would set the exiled Jews free—Cyrus of Persia. Only God could do this. Only God could know a man's name 100 years before he would be born. God makes it very clear that he is the only God. He is the true God, who alone knows the end of everything even before it begins. He is the Lord of all history. People are like flowers or grass. They're here today and gone tomorrow. But God and his word are forever!

(Isaiah 49-61) Isaiah wrote about the Lord's servant. First, it is Israel or Judah who is the "servant of the Lord." But after they failed as his servant, and after they were punished, another "servant of the Lord" would come—Jesus Christ. Isaiah described him *in detail* in Isaiah 53. (Remember, he wrote about Jesus 700 years before Jesus was born.) He said that Jesus would be nothing special when people saw him. Jesus would appear normal. He would be humble and quiet. He would experience suffering and pain. He would even be killed for people's sins. He would die with sinners. (Jesus was crucified with two robbers.) He would be buried with rich people. (Jesus was buried in a rich man's tomb.) But God would raise Jesus again and give him a great reward. Jesus would intercede* for sinners. (Jesus is our High Priest*. He is with God in heaven, interceding for us. See Hebrews 7:24-27 in the *New Testament*.) Isaiah 53 is the clearest statement of the gospel* in the *Old Testament*.

When Jesus opened his ministry on earth, he chose one *Old Testament* scripture to read—Isaiah 61:1-3. Here, the Servant of the Lord is described as one who helps people. Helping people was Jesus' main job while he was here. He still helps us through His spirit in us. (See Luke 4:17-21 in the *New Testament*. See also how Jesus uses Isaiah 61 to answer John the Baptist's followers in Matthew 11:2-6 in the *New Testament*.)

(Isaiah 62-66) One day God will come and judge the world, Isaiah said. God will divide between his people and the evil people. The evil ones will cry out in pain. They will be hungry and thirsty and ashamed. They will be cursed and destroyed. But God's people, those who believe him and follow him, will eat and drink and rejoice. They will take God's name upon themselves. God will bless them forever. Imagine! NO more sorrow or crying or fear or pain forever! God will create a new heaven and earth for us, his people. Praise the Lord! We will live with him forever.

LESSONS FROM ISAIAH

†1 — We are sometimes like the people of Isaiah's day. We go to church, we worship, we feel good, but then we go out and live like the devil during the week. Worship means *nothing* to God if it doesn't come from a heart that tries hard to please him all the time. (Read Isaiah 1.) We can't use church worship to pay for a week of sinning. Sure, we make mistakes. We do sin sometimes. But true worship is when we serve God and serve people for him during the week—not just on Sunday! He wants our worship to come from a pure heart and cleansed mind. Real worship is not in how we raise hands or how we pray or what we sing. Real worship takes place in our hearts. We look at the outside, but God looks at our hearts.

†2 — God's people will win. The end of Isaiah shows us this. So does the book of Revelation and I John in the *New Testament*. "What is the victory that overcomes the world? *Our faith* is the victory!" (See I John 5:4 and 5 in the *New Testament*.) Isaiah wrote about a new heaven and a new earth. Compare what he says in Isaiah 65:17-25 with what John saw in Revelation 21:1-7.

†3 — When I was in graduate school many years ago, I got to read Sennacherib's old, old record of his rule. He names many cities he conquered as he marched. When he gets to Jerusalem in his record, he says, "And I terrified Jerusalem with my great army." He says that because he did not take it, God didn't let him. His record, "Sennacherib's Annals," was written in the ancient language of Aramaic. In those days kings kept careful written records of their rules. (See Esther 6:1 for example.)

JEREMIAH

SUMMARY OF JEREMIAH

(Date of events: about 626-580 B.C.) In Isaiah you learned about Jerusalem, its exile, and its future among the nations of that part of the world. In Jeremiah* you learn much about the hard life of Jeremiah the prophet. You also learn about the end of Jerusalem and the exile of the Jews.

Jeremiah the prophet lived through the last forty years of Jerusalem. The Babylonians had invaded the land of Judah. They broke open Jerusalem's wall of protection and took away the best people of Jerusalem—into exile in Babylon. Jeremiah's job was to preach God's fiery word to the rebellious Jews in Jerusalem. When he preached the word, the people mistreated him terribly. Finally the people forced Jeremiah to go to Egypt, and there he died.

OUTLINE

A. God's call of young Jeremiah (Jeremiah 1)

B. Prophecies against Jerusalem under four kings (Jeremiah 2-25)

C. Jeremiah's hard life and the coming exile (Jeremiah 26-45)

D. Prophecies against other nations (Jeremiah 46-51)

E. The end of Jerusalem (Jeremiah 52)

OVERVIEW

The Book of Jeremiah begins with God's call to Jeremiah. It ends with the destruction of Jerusalem. Everything between the first and last chapter is out of order, time wise. But we can learn more about Jeremiah the prophet than about any other prophet in the *Old Testament*. He had a hard life. He was a priest; so was Ezekiel the prophet. Ezekiel was in Babylon at the same time Jeremiah was in Jerusalem. Jeremiah had very few friends. Baruch, his secretary, was his closest friend. My favorite verses in Jeremiah are 17:9 and 10. He says: "The human heart is so deceitful! It is too sick to be healed. Who can know the heart? 'I the Lord search the heart; I examine the emotions. I reward everyone by the things he does.'" Another favorite verse is Jeremiah 29:11.

Jeremiah warned the leaders of Jerusalem again and again —Jerusalem will be destroyed. The leaders nearly had him killed once. But one of the princes remembered another prophet, Micah; 100 years before Jeremiah, Micah had said, "Jerusalem will be destroyed; it will be plowed up like a farmer's field!" (Micah 3:12) So they didn't kill Jeremiah. They killed another prophet named Uriah, though. They did mistreat Jeremiah. False prophets spoke against him. He was ignored. He was threatened. He was beaten, chained in the temple gates, thrown in prison, put in stocks*, thrown down a muddy cistern*, and finally he was taken by force to Egypt. There, the Jews stoned him to death.

God had Jeremiah do strange things, too.[†1] He told Jeremiah to preach about dirty underwear. He had Jeremiah buy a field. He told Jeremiah not to get married. He made Jeremiah break a clay jar as the leaders watched. Jeremiah wore a wooden yoke*, then an iron one. He cried, especially when his own family tried to kill him. He wrote God's message to King Jehoiakim, but the king cut it up and burned it. So Jeremiah wrote it again, even longer. He was a very shy person, but God made him brave. He even tried not to speak God's word, but he couldn't hold it in long. He said, "When I try not to speak about God, his word becomes like a fire inside my bones! I can't hold it in any longer!" (Jeremiah 20:9) He suffered so much, he wished he'd never been born (Jeremiah 20:14 and 15:10). He tried to get the Jews to surrender to the king of Babylon, because he knew Babylon would finally destroy Jerusalem. But the Jews thought he was a traitor. They believed the lies of all their false prophets, instead of Jeremiah. God finally had to divorce his people, as a husband does an unfaithful wife (Jeremiah 3:8). God gave the Jews so many chances to return to him, but they refused and rebelled. Poor Jeremiah! Like Jesus, Jeremiah finally had to give his life for his people. Jerusalem fell. The Jews were taken to Babylon as slaves, and the book of Jeremiah the prophet ends on a sad note. The Jews were exiled in Babylon for seventy years, just as Jeremiah had said. (See Jeremiah 25:10ff; compare Isaiah 23:15.)

Jeremiah prophesied during the end of Jerusalem, under the last four kings of Jerusalem. He was treated terribly. Jerusalem was destroyed by Babylon's king Nebuchadnezzar. Jeremiah died in Egypt.

LESSONS FROM JEREMIAH

†1 — The Jews had stopped listening, so God had Jeremiah *do* things to get them to listen. Jeremiah did *strange things*:

1. Preached about dirty underwear—(Jeremiah 13) He used this to show the Jews they were like dirty underwear—worthless to God.
2. Bought a field—(Jeremiah 32:6ff) He did this to show the Jews that even though Jerusalem would be destroyed, the Jews *would return* and own land there again.
3. Never married—(Jeremiah 16:2ff) God warned Jeremiah: if he had a wife and children, they would die.
4. Broke a clay jar—(Jeremiah 19) He did this to show the Jews that God would smash Jerusalem.
5. Wore a yoke—(Jeremiah 27 and 28) He did this to show Jerusalem's king that the Jews would be in Babylon for seventy years. Jeremiah also cursed a false prophet. That prophet died two months later.

There are many other strange and interesting things in Jeremiah. Did you know that God had been divorced? Whenever you feel pain, remember that God felt pain, too. Divorce is a very painful thing. God knows how you feel when you hurt. (God *divorced* Israel, then Judah. See Jeremiah 3:6-13.)

LAMENTATIONS

SUMMARY OF LAMENTATIONS

(Date of writing: about 585 B.C.) In Jeremiah you learned about Jeremiah's hard life and the destruction of Jerusalem. In Lamentations* you learn how Jeremiah cried over Jerusalem's destruction and how he trusted God for the future.

Jeremiah the prophet cried again and again. He saw horrible things happening in Jerusalem just before its destruction. Lamentations records Jeremiah crying over Jerusalem.

OUTLINE

A. Jerusalem sinned and now cries (Lamentations 1)

B. The Lord punished Jerusalem (Lamentations 2)

C. The Lord did not forgive, but he is faithful (Lamentations 3)

D. Jerusalem's terrible punishment (Lamentations 4)

E. Jeremiah prays for God's help (Lamentations 5)

OVERVIEW

Jeremiah wrote Lamentations right after Jerusalem fell. The city was in ruins because of the people's sins. The city walls were torn down by the Babylonians. Some people in Jerusalem starved to death. Others boiled and ate their own children! Women were raped and killed.

Leaders were hung up by their hands. Some were killed and others went away into exile as slaves. Many died of diseases. Some were burned to death.

Jeremiah thought of God as Job did—as the enemy. God is the one who punished the Jews. All the Jews still alive were bowed down with sorrow. How horrible they all felt! Their enemies killed the priests and prophets and tore down God's temple. The Jewish religion was destroyed. The temple would not be rebuilt for seventy years. All this happened because the Jews sinned so much against God. But Jeremiah knew God still loved his people, even though he punished them. Jeremiah still hoped for God's blessings. (See Lamentations 3:22ff.) No matter how bad things are, God *will* one day bless his people.

EZEKIEL

SUMMARY OF EZEKIEL

(Date of events: about 595-570 B.C.) Ezekiel the prophet lived during the fall of Jerusalem. Unlike Jeremiah, Ezekiel prophesied in Babylon. He had been taken prisoner several years before Jerusalem was destroyed. Like Jeremiah, Ezekiel was both a prophet and a priest. His book is one of the strangest in the *Old Testament*, but at least it is in order, time wise. He prophesied to the other Jewish slaves in exile in Babylon. He prophesied for about twenty years.

OUTLINE

A. Warnings: the fall of Jerusalem (Ezekiel 1-24)

B. Warnings: other nations will fall (Ezekiel 25-32)

C. Promises: God will bless his people (Ezekiel 33-48)

OVERVIEW

The Babylonians captured Ezekiel with many other Jews from Jerusalem. They took him to Babylon. He had been in exile about four years when God called him. He saw a strange vision of God riding on a cherub*. God grabbed Ezekiel by the hair, lifted him up, and took him for a ride on the cherub! He took Ezekiel to Jerusalem, 1,000 miles away, in an instant! (See Ezekiel 8:1ff.) Ezekiel saw what was happening in Jerusalem. Then he told the exiles (the Jews in Babylon) what was happening in Jerusalem. He told them by acting out strange things.[t1] God told Ezekiel several strange things to do to teach the Jews in Babylon. God wanted them to know that he was with them even that far away. He also wanted them to know that Jerusalem was going to be destroyed for sure. He told the people: "Even if three good men, Noah, Daniel*, and Job, were in Jerusalem, the city would still be destroyed!" (See Ezekiel 14:12ff.) Jerusalem and its people were evil, so God was forced to destroy them. God will punish, but he is always ready to forgive. (See Ezekiel 33:11.)

God warned Ezekiel that on the day Jerusalem was destroyed Ezekiel's wife would die (Ezekiel 24:15ff). God told Ezekiel, "Don't cry!" It happened as God had said. Like Jeremiah, Ezekiel had to suffer. He had to know how God felt, so he could speak for God. From Ezekiel, the Jews knew about the fall of Jerusalem before the news of its fall was brought to them. Then they knew Ezekiel was really a prophet of God.

Although Ezekiel had much to say about the destruction of other nations (chapters 25-32), most of his preaching was to the Jews. He warned the people that each one was responsible for his own sin. (See Ezekiel 33:10-20.) God was especially angry with the Jewish leaders (Ezekiel 34). These "shepherds" had hurt their "sheep" (the Jews) instead of helping them. God promises that he will one day give his people one shepherd, the *Good Shepherd*, (Jesus) who will care for them the *right* way.[t2]

(Ezekiel 38-39) Ezekiel says a lot of things in symbols. He says that God's people will be attacked by the world around them, but God will finally save his people and destroy their enemies.

(Ezekiel 40-48) One day God will build a new temple, Ezekiel says. An angel came to Ezekiel to measure this new temple in Ezekiel's vision. The angel measured and measured and measured, for about nine chapters. This is to show us that this new temple will be *holy*. (Measuring in the Bible often means that God is making something holy.) A great river[t3] will flow out of the new temple. The land around this temple will be for all God's people. No one will ever take our land from us again. And we will have a great city to live in. The name of the city is "The Lord is there." (This city is heaven. See Revelation 21 in the *New Testament*. Also see Hebrews 11:10, 16 and 12:22, and 13:14.)

LESSONS FROM EZEKIEL

†1 — To get the Jews in Babylon to pay attention, Ezekiel did strange things: (Symbols)

1. Ate a scroll—(Ezekiel 3:1ff) God put his words into Ezekiel's mouth. The scroll tasted sweet in his mouth, because God's word is sweet. (See Psalm 19:10.) But God's word can also be hard and painful. (See Revelation 10:9-10 in the *New Testament*.)

2. Played army—(Ezekiel 4:1ff) Ezekiel drew a map of Jerusalem on a brick. He built little toy war machines around the brick. He shook his fist at the brick and preached against it. He was acting out Babylon's attack on Jerusalem and God's anger at Jerusalem.

3. Got a haircut—(Ezekiel 5:1ff) He took his hair and divided it into three equal piles. Then he took a tiny pinch of it and wrapped it in his clothes. One pile of hair he chopped up with a sword; one pile he burned; one pile he scattered in the wind. This was to show the Jews in Babylon what God was doing to the people in Jerusalem. The tiny pinch was the remnant*, the few Jews God would save.

4. Cut a hole in the wall—(Ezekiel 12:5ff) Ezekiel packed a bag of clothes and made a big hole in the wall of his house. He went through the hole with the bag. This was to show the people how the Jews in Jerusalem were trying to escape from the Babylonian army. But they would not escape.

5. Trembled—(Ezekiel 12:17ff) Ezekiel pretended to be afraid; the Jews could see him shaking. This was to show them that the Jews in Jerusalem were terrified. They would soon be destroyed.

There are many other signs and strange stories in Ezekiel to help teach the truth to God's people in Babylon. For example, see Ezekiel 4:9ff, Ezekiel 15, 17, and others.

†2 — The Good Shepherd, David: See Ezekiel 34:23 and 37:24, where Ezekiel calls the good shepherd "David." Of course, David had been dead about 400 years when Ezekiel said that. See also John 10:11ff in the *New Testament*. "David" means *one who is loved*. Often Jesus is called "David" in the prophets. (See Jeremiah 30:9 and 33:21; Hosea 3:5; Amos 9:11.)

†3 — (Ezekiel 47:1-12) The great river is a symbol for the Holy Spirit of God. God will cause his Holy Spirit to flow out of the new temple (which is the Church, the body of Christ) and bring life wherever the Spirit reaches! (See John 2:19 in the *New Testament*, where Jesus is talking about his own body.)

DANIEL

SUMMARY OF DANIEL

(Date of events: about 606-530 B.C.) Daniel the prophet was taken captive by the Babylonians before Jerusalem was destroyed. All his adult life was spent in Babylon. He prophesied to several rulers there for about seventy years. Daniel's prophecies are about worldwide events and how they affect Jerusalem.

OUTLINE

A. Events in Daniel's life (Daniel 1-6)
B. Daniel's visions of the future (Daniel 7-12)

OVERVIEW

(Daniel 1) Daniel and many other young men were taken to Babylon. He and his three friends, Shadrach, Meshach, and Abed-nego, refused to eat the king's rich food. They asked permission to eat whole grains, fruit, and vegetables.[†1] After ten days the four young men looked healthier and stronger than all the others. So all four of them became members of the king's royal council. They gave better advice to King Nebuchadnezzar than any other counselors.

(Daniel 2) King Nebuchadnezzar of Babylon had a dream. He couldn't remember it, but he just *knew* it was important. He demanded that his counselors tell him what he dreamed and what it meant. Of course, they couldn't know the king's dream unless he told them. He threatened them: "If you don't tell me the dream *and* its meaning, I'll have all of you destroyed!" But Daniel prayed, and God told him both the dream *and* its meaning.[t2] He told King Nebuchadnezzar, and the king was happy again. He trusted Daniel and made him to be head over Babylon. Like Joseph in Egypt, only the king himself was above Daniel. (See Genesis 41:40.)

(Daniel 3) King Nebuchadnezzar made a huge gold idol and made everyone worship the idol. But Daniel's three friends refused to bow down to an idol. The king had them thrown into a fiery furnace.[t3] The fire was so hot that the soldiers who threw the three young men in were killed. But when King Nebuchadnezzar looked in, he saw Daniel's three friends walking around in the furnace unhurt. And there was another person in there who looked like "a son of the gods," as Nebuchadnezzar put it. The three friends walked out of that fire unhurt. Even their clothes didn't smell like smoke! The king was amazed. He then moved the three friends to a higher place in Babylon.

(Daniel 4) Nebuchadnezzar had another dream, and Daniel told him it was a warning. Daniel said, "You will become like an animal if you don't stop sinning." Nebuchadnezzar's worst sin was his pride. One year later Nebuchadnezzar really did become like an animal for seven years.[t4] When he got his mind back, he worshipped God instead of himself!

(Daniel 5) Years later another king's son, Belshazzar by name, had a party. The people at the party got drunk on wine. They were drinking out of the cups that came from God's temple at Jerusalem. Suddenly, they all saw fingers writing a message on the wall. The message was something like this:

```
M  M  T  U
N  N  K  Ph
E  E  E  A
      L  R
         S
         I
         N
```

No one could tell what it meant, until Daniel came. He told Belshazzar he was about to lose his kingdom. Sure enough, that night Belshazzar was killed, and Darius the Mede took over as king.

(Daniel 6) Daniel was an old man, one of the greatest in Darius' kingdom. Some other leaders were jealous of Daniel. So they helped King Darius make a new rule: "No one can ask anyone but King Darius for anything." But Daniel went on and prayed to God as usual. His enemies reported this to Darius. They said, "Daniel is asking his God for something, King Darius!" Darius did not want to, but he had to enforce the new law. He had to throw Daniel into a pit of lions. The king worried about Daniel all night long, but he didn't need to. God protected Daniel. The next day King Darius saw that Daniel was alright. Darius was so angry that he threw all Daniel's enemies to the lions, and the lions killed them all. King Darius the Mede worshipped Daniel's God, too.

(Daniel 7) Daniel had a dream about strange animals coming out of the ocean. The first animal (a lion with wings) stood for Babylon. The second (a bear) stood for the second empire, Medo-Persia. The third animal (a leopard with four wings) stood for the Greek empire, and the fourth (an awful-looking animal) stood for Rome. So God showed Daniel the empires that would rule the world over the next 1,000 years or so. During the fourth empire (Rome), God would start his kingdom (the church).

Daniel 8-12 contains some of the most exact and accurate prophecies* in the Bible. God showed Daniel what would happen in the next five or six centuries. These chapters are so detailed and complicated that it is better to study the rest of the prophets first. If you try to understand Daniel 8-12, you may have problems. Even Daniel did! (See Daniel 8:27, 10:1, and 12:8.)

LESSONS FROM DANIEL

†1 — The food Daniel asked for was "seeds," the most nutritious of all foods. In my class on the Hebrew prophets, I spend one full day on nutrition—teaching about vitamins, minerals, and foods. It has always been interesting to me that God shortened the life of people

and at about the same time told them they could eat meat! (Genesis 6:3 and 9:3.) (Before the flood, people lived a *long* time and ate no meat—see Genesis 5.) My suggestions for a healthy diet are:

1. Eat very little fat and no blood.
2. Eat lots of vegetables and fruit. Raw is best.
3. Eat lots of whole grains: wheat, rye, barley, rice, etc.
4. Take a multivitamin and minerals, with lots of vitamin C with meals. (Vitamins and minerals help form the acids that digest your food.)
5. Drink lots of pure water (eight large glasses daily).
6. Get plenty of sleep (nine hours or so is best).

†2 — Daniel told the king that he would know the dream *and* its meaning the next day. That night Daniel prayed *hard* for God to tell him. God did. Don't you think Daniel had a *lot* of faith in God?

Daniel 2 and Daniel 7 are two different visions with exactly the same meaning. Like the two dreams of Pharaoh in Egypt, so these two visions reveal the future. God gives *two* visions, because it is *certain*. (See Genesis 41:32.)

†3 — The fiery furnace was a lime-kiln, a very hot place for melting metals. It had an opening at the top and the bottom, like a giant fireplace. The three men were probably thrown in the top, where the heat going up killed the soldiers. The king probably looked in the door at the bottom to see the four men walking in the fire.

†4 — The disease Nebuchadnezzar got is known today as *lycanthropy*. This word is from Greek. It means *wolfman*. Maybe this is where the idea of the *werewolf* comes from. Look up lycanthropy in a medical dictionary or a good encyclopedia. It is a real disease, even today.

HOSEA

SUMMARY OF HOSEA

(Date of events: about 750-710 B.C.) Hosea the Prophet married a prostitute, Gomer by name. Hosea was a faithful husband, but Gomer was unfaithful to him. Hosea was like God, and Gomer was like Israel. Hosea felt all the pain that God felt because of unfaithful Israel. So he was able to speak for God to the northern kingdom—Israel. He prophesied up to and during the end of the northern kingdom, when Assyria conquered Israel and took them away into exile.

OUTLINE

A. Hosea marries a prostitute (Hosea 1-3)

B. Hosea warns Israel about destruction (Hosea 4-13)

C. A promise for the future (Hosea 14)

OVERVIEW

The people of Israel were so sexually sinful that God did something very unusual to Hosea. He told Hosea to marry a prostitute and have children with her! Hosea married Gomer and she had three children. Hosea knew that her first child was his. The second child may have been his; Hosea was not sure. The third child was not his. Like Israel, Gomer was being unfaithful. Israel worshipped idols, and Gomer had sex with other men. God loved Israel and Hosea loved Gomer, so God and Hosea felt the same kind of pain. Both were hurt by their unfaithful wives. (Israel was God's wife; see Hosea 2:19 and 3:1.) God told Hosea to go get Gomer back from her lovers, just as God planned to take Israel back from the idols. Hosea bought his wife back and took her out to the desert, away from all her lovers. He separated Gomer from her men friends until she finally wanted to have sex with him again. In the same way, God would use Assyria to conquer Israel. Assyria took Israel away into exile, so one day Israel would want God back again. God wanted Hosea to understand how God felt, so he could speak God's word to his "prostitute" people. Like Jeremiah later on, Hosea had a life of pain. Israel had no excuse. They could not say, "I didn't know," because Hosea made sure they *did* know. Hosea was the last prophet of the northern kingdom.

JOEL

SUMMARY OF JOEL

(Date of events: about 850 B.C.) In my opinion, Joel is the earliest of all the writing prophets. (Other writers say Joel was written later.) He prophesies during a plague of locusts. He uses the locust plague to warn Judah about God's coming judgement, which he calls "The Day of the Lord."

OUTLINE

A. The locust plague; repent (Joel 1:1-2:17)

B. Judah's salvation: the future "Day of the Lord" (Joel 2:18-3:21)

OVERVIEW

Some people believe that some other prophets sometimes copied from Joel. The "Day of the Lord" is a time of judgment and blessing. Joel uses the phrase "Day of the Lord" in four different ways:

1. The plague of locusts (Joel 1:4)

2. An invading army (Joel 2:2ff)

3. The beginning of the Church (Joel 2:28ff)

4. The end of the world (Joel 3)

a. The locust plague is a sign for the first "Day of the Lord." The locusts destroyed all their crops. The people of Judah were very afraid of this natural disaster.

b. The invading army (chapter 2) is probably just a description of the locusts. Joel tells the town watchman to blow the trumpet to warn Jerusalem of the locust invasion, just as if the locusts were an army. Joel tells all the Jews in Judah to repent—the drunks, the farmers, even the priests!

c. The future *Day of the Lord* will be wonderful for God's people. God promises to pour out His Holy Spirit on all people—even slaves! This is new for the Jews. It has never happened before. In the *Old Testament*, only kings, prophets, and priests had God's Spirit. Now all people will have God living in them. This prediction was fulfilled in Acts 2. Peter the apostle* stood up and preached the first Gospel sermon, based on Joel 2:28-32. That day the "wind of the spirit" roared down on God's people! (Read Acts 2:1-36 in the *New Testament*.) Now all believers in Jesus have God's Spirit.

d. The end of the world will be terrifying for all who reject the Lord. But God's people will be safe and secure. (See especially Joel 3:12-21.)

AMOS

SUMMARY OF AMOS

(Date of events: about 750 B.C.) Amos was a prophet to the northern kingdom, Israel. He said that everyone who belongs to God should treat other people right. But the people of Israel did not care. The rich Israelites treated the poor ones like dogs. They even made fathers into slaves just to buy shoes for their children. (See Amos 2:6.) Besides that, the Jews in Israel were sexually immoral all the time. Amos, like the other prophets, says, "Repent, or you will be destroyed!"

OUTLINE

A. God is angry with many nations (Amos 1-2)

B. God is angry with Israel. Repent! (Amos 3-6)

C. God will punish Israel. Exile! (Amos 7:1-9:10)

D. Hope for the future (Amos 9:11-15)

OVERVIEW

Amos was a gardener and a shepherd. He lived in Judah, the southern kingdom. But God called him to preach to Israel, the northern kingdom. He had a very short time of service. He preached to Israel about the same time as Hosea, but Hosea served a long time. Amos is the prophet of "social justice." He commanded the Israelites to stop cheating each other, to stop sinning sexually, to repent! But the people were hard hearted. They refused to obey. So Amos warned them that God would bring terrible punishment on them. The lucky ones would become slaves and go into exile. The others would certainly be killed. Amos says, "It will be like a man running from a lion, only to run into a bear. If he got away from both and hid in his own house, even there a cobra would bite him." (Amos 5:19) In other words, Amos says that there is no escape! God will destroy them for their evil deeds. All Amos got from the Israelites was, "Get out of here! Stop preaching here!" (Amos 7:12ff) But he would not leave. He would not stop preaching. "God will destroy you!" he said (Amos 9:8). But one day in the future, God will bless his people. (See Amos 9:11-15.)

OBADIAH

SUMMARY OF OBADIAH

(Date of events: probably about 850 or 600 B.C.) Obadiah's name means *worshipper of the Lord*, but his book is so short people know very little about him. He promises that God will destroy Edom.

OUTLINE

A. Edom* will be destroyed (Obadiah 1-14)

B. All nations will be punished (Obadiah 15-18)

C. God's people will survive (Obadiah 19-21)

OVERVIEW

Obadiah's tiny book is about the tribe of Esau, Jacob's twin brother. God promises that Edom (Esau's tribe) will be destroyed. The nations who pretend to be friends of Edom will attack Edom. The Edomites* made slaves of their cousins, the Jews, so Edom will be punished. No one from Edom will be left alive; all Edomites will die! But God will one day save his people, Obadiah promises.

JONAH

SUMMARY OF JONAH

(Date of events: probably about 725 B.C.) Jonah ran away when God asked him to go to Nineveh*, the capital city of Assyria, to preach repentance. He took a ship across the Mediterranean Sea. He was thrown in the sea. A great fish swallowed Jonah, then spit him out three days later. Then Jonah obeyed God and went to Nineveh. He was angry when God did not destroy Nineveh. God taught Jonah a lesson about love for all people.

OUTLINE

   A. Jonah runs from God (Jonah 1)

   B. Jonah runs to God in prayer (Jonah 2)

   C. Jonah runs with God and preaches (Jonah 3)

   D. Jonah runs ahead of God and is angry (Jonah 4)

OVERVIEW

Jonah's name means *dove*. Like a dove, Jonah tried to "fly away" when God spoke to him. God asked Jonah the prophet to travel to Nineveh, the capital city of Assyria. God wanted Jonah to warn the people that Nineveh would soon be destroyed if they did not repent of their bad ways.

But Jonah hated all people who were not Jews. Especially Assyrians. The Assyrians were Gentiles* and very evil and violent people. So Jonah got on a ship headed for Spain, clear across the Mediterranean Sea. The ship set out, but a great storm came up. The sailors threw everything off the ship so it wouldn't sink. When the storm grew even stronger, the sailors began praying to their gods. Finally, they were desperate. They rolled dice to see whose fault the storm was. The dice pointed to Jonah. Jonah knew then that God was causing the storm. He told the sailors to throw him into the sea. When they did, the storm stopped. The sailors then worshipped the true God.

God had prepared a huge fish to swallow Jonah! When Jonah was inside the fish, he prayed to God. Then the Lord made the fish spit Jonah up on land. Then God told Jonah a second time to go to Nineveh. This time Jonah obeyed. I think I would, too! So Jonah made the long trip to Nineveh. When he got there, he told them, "In forty days, Nineveh will be destroyed!" The people believed Jonah, and they repented. To show God they were serious, they did not eat or drink anything. God saw their change of heart, so he called off their destruction.

Jonah got angry at God. He wanted God to destroy Nineveh and all its people. Jonah went up on a hill in the shade and sat down. He wanted to see God destroy the city. God caused worms to eat the plant Jonah was under. The plant died, so Jonah was in the hot sunlight. God even made a hot wind blow on Jonah. Jonah was mad enough at God to die, he said. But God tried to teach Jonah not to be so prejudiced[†1]. God loved the people of Nineveh, even if they weren't Jews.

LESSONS FROM JONAH

[†1] — A bigot is a person who hates certain kinds of people. Jonah was a bigot. He was prejudiced against anyone who wasn't Jewish. He *hated* Gentiles, and the Assyrians were some of the worst of the Gentiles. He had no mercy. He really wanted to see the fireworks when God destroyed Nineveh. But God taught him a lesson about love.

God was willing to use even a bigot like Jonah. This gives me hope! God can even use a person with problems. Maybe he can use even me or even you.

Jonah is just one way that the Bible is honest with us. The Bible reveals Jonah's prejudice very clearly. But God loves everyone. We should, too. Jesus even said, "Love your enemies." (See Matthew 5:43-48 in the *New Testament*.) God can help us overcome our prejudices if we let him.

MICAH

SUMMARY OF MICAH

(Date of events: probably about 730 to 690 B.C.) In Jonah you learned about a rebel prophet who hated Gentiles. In Micah you learn about a man who preached to farmers in the southern kingdom. Micah preached a lot like Isaiah. He preached in the country of Judea, while Isaiah preached in Jerusalem. He preached to the poor; Isaiah mainly preached to the kings' families.

OUTLINE

A. Israel's sin and punishment (Micah 1-3)

B. Israel's future peace (Micah 4)

C. Jesus Christ will be our peace (Micah 5)

D. What God really wants (Micah 6)

E. Warning and thanks (Micah 7)

OVERVIEW

Micah probably knew Isaiah the Prophet. He must have heard him speak, because he quotes one of Isaiah's sermons. (Micah 4:1-3 is like Isaiah 2:1-4.)

Micah lived in the country not too far from Jerusalem. He could see that the northern kingdom had been destroyed by Assyria. In fact, the Assyrian army came and surrounded Jerusalem! (See Micah 1:9 and compare Isaiah 36 and 37.) He warned Jerusalem that they would be destroyed in the future if they did not repent. He said, "Stop hurting the poor. Start helping them. Stop listening to these false prophets who preach for money. Listen to me! I speak for God." He said, "Because of your sins, Jerusalem will be plowed up like a farmer's field!" (See Micah 3:12.) But Israel will have a great future. God will bring his people back from the exile. He will send a ruler who lives forever. This ruler will give God's people peace. (The ruler is Jesus Christ.) Micah even tells the people where Jesus will be born—Bethlehem! (See Micah 5:2 and context.)

What does God really want us to do? How should we live? Micah answers in 6:8: "What God wants are three things: first, he wants us to treat all people with love. (This is what *justice* means.) Second, God wants us to be his friends. (This is what *mercy* means; it really means we should be careful to keep our covenant with him.) Third, God wants us to live simple, humble lives, as we share our lives with him. God doesn't want us to give animals or wealth as sacrifices. What he really wants is *us*. What Micah is saying in 6:8 is what all the *Old Testament* teaches. We should love God and love people. We should help anyone who needs help. Everything God has done for us is to get us to love him! This is the meaning of the Bible. Micah really did understand God.

NAHUM

SUMMARY OF NAHUM

(Date of writing: sometime before 612 B.C.) In Micah you learned what God really wants of us. In Nahum* you learn that the capital of Assyria, Nineveh, is about to fall. Nahum had a vision of Nineveh's destruction before it happened. He tells us about it in his little book.

OUTLINE

A. God will destroy Nineveh but save his people (Nahum 1)

B. Nineveh's destruction (Nahum 2 and 3)

OVERVIEW

Israel, the northern kingdom, had been destroyed nearly 100 years before. Nahum preached to the southern kingdom, Judah. Judah would later be carried away to exile, but Nahum promised that the future for Judah would be good. The future for Nineveh would be destruction. The people of Nineveh had repented once, long ago, after Jonah preached there. But this time they would not repent. Nineveh was evil. They murdered people for the fun of it. The raped and stole in other nations. They were very cruel. Everyone knew how evil they were. So God had decided to destroy Nineveh. Nahum saw in a vision that Babylon's army would attack Nineveh and win the war. Babylon's army was God's punishment on Nineveh. There were so many dead bodies in Nineveh that the people stumbled over them! (See Nahum 3:3 and context.)

HABAKKUK

SUMMARY OF HABAKKUK

(Date of writing: probably about 610 B.C.) In Nahum you learned about the destruction of Nineveh. In Habakkuk* you learn that faith in God will make us right with him. Babylon will destroy Jerusalem and the temple (Habakkuk 1 and 2). But God will come with great power and crush the enemies of his people (Habakkuk 3).

OUTLINE

A. Why the Lord lets bad people seem to destroy good people (Habakkuk 1 and 2)

B. What God will do for his people when he comes (Habakkuk 3)

OVERVIEW

Babylon, an enemy of God's people, came into the promised land. This enemy was oppressing God's people. Habakkuk complained to God about it. He said, "God, you are holy and you live forever. Why are you letting our enemy oppress us? They are even more evil than we are!" God answered: "It may seem like evil people are hurting good people now. But in the future there will be good news. Evil people will die, but good people will live. *They will live because they believe in me.*" This is a great answer! In fact, the *New Testament* books of Romans and Galatians are based on this statement. *Good people will live because they believe God's message, the Gospel.* (See Habakkuk 2:4.) Enemies may seem to hurt or destroy God's people now, but God will keep his people safe, no matter what happens!

Read Habakkuk's prayer in Habakkuk 3. Then you will know what great power God has! God may let his people suffer for a while in *this* life. But one day he will save us all and protect us forever. So we can live a happy and confident life, even if bad things happen to us. How can we be happy even in bad times? Our God will win, and he is on *our* side. (Read Romans 8:31 in the *New Testament*.) Even if we are *killed*, we will live again! God said so.

ZEPHANIAH

SUMMARY OF ZEPHANIAH

(Date of writing: probably sometime around 610 B.C. or earlier.) In Habakkuk you learned of a prophet who trusted God even in bad times. In Zephaniah* you learn of another prophet who trusted God to protect him even though judgment day was coming. He saw that Babylon would come down and destroy Jerusalem and the nations around it. But God would protect the people who were sincerely sorry for their sin.

OUTLINE

A. God will punish Jerusalem (Zephaniah 1)

B. Worldwide sin and punishment (Zephaniah 2:1-3:8)

C. Worldwide joy and blessing in the future (Zephaniah 3:9-20)

OVERVIEW

Zephaniah was in the family of the king of Jerusalem. He told the people of Jerusalem that God would destroy anyone who worshipped false gods. "God will send Babylon to kill all you sinners and idol worshippers," he says. But the people of Jerusalem didn't even believe in God. So he warned them: "God is so angry with you! Your blood will gush out like water! No amount of money will save you." But even then, Zephaniah offers hope to them: "If you repent and turn to the

Lord, he may protect you in the day of destruction." Zephaniah told them that when their enemies were killed, they would be, too. All the cities of the land will be left empty. Wild animals and wild birds would be the only things left alive in the cities. The people would be gone, either killed or taken away to be slaves in Babylon.

But God has a shining future for those who obey him. All the Gentiles and Jews who follow God will be saved.[t1] In the future, all people who love the Lord will sing and shout for joy! (Read Zephaniah 3:14-20.)

LESSONS FROM ZEPHANIAH

[t1] — Even in the *Old Testament*, God's message is for all peoples, not just the Jews. Zephaniah said that God would change the Gentiles' hearts, too. The Gentiles and Jews who worship and serve God will one day be happy and rich, afraid of nothing. (Read Zephaniah 3:9-13.) In the *New Testament*, Romans 3:22ff says there is no difference between Jew and Gentile, because all are sinners. Romans 11:32 says that all people are prisoners of disobedience, so God can show love to everyone. And Galatians 3:28f makes it even clearer. Paul says that all differences mean nothing. All that matters is that you follow Jesus!

HAGGAI

SUMMARY OF HAGGAI

(Date of writing: about 520 B.C.) In Zephaniah you learned about a prophet of Jerusalem. He warned the people of Jerusalem's coming destruction. In Haggai you learn of a prophet after the exile. Haggai wants the Jews to finish building the new temple.

OUTLINE

A. Lazy people are not blessed by God (Haggai 1)
B. Build God's temple! (Haggai 2)

OVERVIEW

(Haggai 1) Haggai's name means *party*. His parents must have been believers, so they named him that happy name. They thought the seventy-year exile was about over, and Haggai would be back in Jerusalem for the party at the Jews' return. But when the Jews returned, they built their own houses instead of God's temple. Haggai told them that the bad weather they were having was from God. He said God wanted them to stop working on their houses and start working on *His*. So the people were sorry and began to work on the temple.

(Haggai 2) Some of the old people could remember the temple of Solomon from before the exile. These people were very disappointed by this new temple. Nothing would ever be as great as Solomon's temple. But God told Haggai that one day his temple would be filled with the wealth of all the nations. God said "temple," but he was really referring to heaven. God said, "One day I will shake the heavens and the earth." (See Haggai 2:6f and 21f.) One day all the wealth and kingdoms of the world will belong to God and Jesus! (See also Hebrews 12:26f in the *New Testament*.)

ZECHARIAH

SUMMARY OF ZECHARIAH

(Date of writing: about 520 to 470 B.C.) In Haggai you learned about a prophet who got the Jews in Jerusalem to rebuild the temple. In Zechariah* you learn about a strange prophet. He promised that God would judge the world, but God's people would be greatly blessed.

OUTLINE

A. Eight visions of future fear and joy for God's people (Zechariah 1-8)

B. The coming of God's shepherd-king, and peace for God's people (Zechariah 9-14)

OVERVIEW

Zechariah was a young man. He was both a prophet and a priest, like Jeremiah and Ezekiel had been. His message to the Jews is very clear; God said, "Return to me and I will return to you!" (See Zechariah 1:3.) God gave eight visions to Zechariah.[†1] All of them were in symbols; all of them were to get the Jews to return to God. They call the Jews to repent, to return to Jerusalem, to build the temple, and to serve God. The first and last of the eight visions are very similar.

The name Zechariah uses for God is *Lord Sabaoth*, which means *Lord of armies*. It is a mighty name for God, showing his power over all the universe, whether physical or spiritual. He uses this name nearly fifty times in the book. (Some modern versions have it, "The Lord Almighty." Old versions have "The Lord of Hosts.") It points to God's total control over everything.

THE VISIONS:

1. (1:7-17) The horseman and horses in the trees: a vision of worldwide peace with God's blessing on his people. But God will punish Israel's enemies. God controls all the world.

2. (1:18-21) The four horns and four workmen: a vision of God's punishment on all the nations that hurt his people. (Compare this vision to Daniel 2 and 7 in the *Old Testament*.)

3. (Zechariah 2) A man to measure Jerusalem: the new Jerusalem will not need to be measured; it will be full of too many people to measure. God himself will protect Jerusalem and punish those who hurt it. "Rejoice, Jerusalem, because God will again choose you!"

4. (Zechariah 3) Clean clothes for Joshua the high priest: the Lord will purify his people on a single day. God will purify Israel's religion. This vision symbolically shows God taking away sin and guilt and disarming Satan. God's servant, the Branch,[t2] will give us peace.

5. (Zechariah 4) The gold candlestick and two olive trees: Zechariah gets the people excited to rebuild God's temple. He does this by showing them God's eternal and powerful Holy Spirit. The symbol of the Spirit is a seven-pronged candlestick. God's power is behind the Jews. He gives them the power to build the temple, through his Spirit. (See Zechariah 4:6.)

6. (Zechariah 5:1-4) The flying book: God will remove all the worst sinners from the land.

7. (Zechariah 5:5-11) A woman inside a basket: not only will God remove repeat offenders (people who keep on sinning) from this land; he will also take away all that is not right from the land. God's land will be holy, but the enemy's land will be full of evil.

8. (Zechariah 6:1-8) Four horses and chariots: God's judgement will come upon the earth again and again. In this way God pays back Israel's enemies for their sins against Israel.

(Zechariah 6:9-15) Now Zechariah explains the real meaning of the third and fourth visions about Joshua and Jerusalem. The coming Priest King (Jesus Christ) will "build the Temple." "Build the Temple" may be a symbol for Jesus' body, and then for his Church. (See John 2:19-22 and Matthew 27:40 in the *New Testament*. Also see Ephesians 4:12ff and Romans 12:4f in the *New Testament*.)

The rest of Zechariah is very symbolic. God promises future blessings on Jerusalem, but judgment on the enemies of his people. Zechariah promises that King Jesus, when he comes, will be humble. (See 9:9ff.) God will punish the evil leaders of his people and replace them with Jesus, the Good Shepherd. The Good Shepherd will be killed to make his people clean (chapters 12 and 13). Then one day God will destroy his enemies. He will end war forever. He will rule over all the nations who worship him.

LESSONS FROM ZECHARIAH

[1] — All these visions are symbolic. They tell us that the exile in Babylon is over. The temple will be rebuilt, and the Priest King will come. God will then remove sin from his people; people of all nations will come to him, and he will save them. Many of these visions are used again in a different way in the Book of Revelation in the *New Testament*. (For example, see the "seven-pronged candlestick" in Revelation 1:20.)

"Jerusalem" in Zechariah is often like "Jerusalem" in the Book of Revelation in the *New Testament*. It is not the Jerusalem in Israel; it is not "earthly" Jerusalem. Earthly Jerusalem is called "Sodom and Egypt" in Revelation 11:8. (See also Isaiah 1:9f and Jeremiah 23:14.) God hated Sodom and destroyed it (Genesis 19:24ff). Of course, he also destroyed Egypt's power (Exodus 14:23-28). Earthly Jerusalem will be like that—destroyed. But Zechariah and Revelation often speak of a "spiritual" Jerusalem or "heavenly" Jerusalem. (See especially Revelation 21:1-4.) This *new* Jerusalem is what Christians hope for. One day you will be with God there. The new Jerusalem is also spoken of in Psalm 46:4f and Hebrews 11:10 and 16, 12:22, and 13:14 and all of Revelation 21 and 22 in the *New Testament*.)

The numbers of these visions are very important. These numbers will be explained in Book II of *The Bible for Busy People*. See the chapter on the Book of Revelation.

†2 — The Branch is often a symbol for Jesus. See Isaiah 11:1 and 10; Isaiah 53:2; Jeremiah 23:5 and 33:15; Zechariah 3:8 and 6:12.

MALACHI

SUMMARY OF MALACHI

(Date of events: probably about 430 B.C.) Malachi* is the last prophet of the *Old Testament*. After his book there are no more prophets until John the Baptist, 400 years later.

The leaders and people were not living for God or giving to God's work. Malachi was like many other prophets. He called the people back to God. Malachi said that later on someone would prepare the way for the Lord to come.

OUTLINE

A. The Lord is faithful, but Israel is not (Malachi 1-2)

B. Repent, for the Lord is coming (Malachi 3-4)

OVERVIEW

(Malachi 1) Malachi says the Lord is great the world over. He is not limited just to Israel! So why don't you priests obey God? Why don't you honor him? Something is wrong in the hearts of those who give worthless gifts to God. God sees beyond the gifts into the worshippers' hearts. He knows when people care or don't care. In Malachi's day, the priests didn't care. But people all over the world honor God. He is not a small god, limited to the Jewish nation. He is God Almighty, over *all* nations!

(Malachi 2) God will pay back the priests if they don't start doing right. He will bring punishment on them if they don't change. The priests have broken God's covenant, so God will make them wish they had obeyed.

Then God speaks to the people. "I hate divorce," God says. When a man promises his wife to be faithful, the man should keep his promise! God hates it when people don't keep their word. He hates divorce, because it *hurts* so much. Anyone who has been divorced knows the terrible pain of it. So we should always keep our promises to others. What would it be like if *God* didn't keep *his* promises?

(Malachi 3) God says, "I will send my messenger to prepare my way." John the Baptist is that messenger. (See Mark 1:1-8 in the *New Testament*.) He comes 400 years after Malachi. John the Baptist will be like "strong soap" or like "fire to purify metal." (See Malachi 3:2f.) He will condemn evil people and praise the good ones. (See especially Mark 6:17-20 in the *New Testament*.) John was not a weakling. He was a strong leader!

God speaks through Malachi. He says, "If you don't cheat me, if you bring me one tenth of all your money and food, I will give you a great blessing, too big for you to carry away!" If we do what God wants, if we give our best to him, he will really give us good things. He will have mercy on us; we will be his people, and he will care for us.

(Malachi 4) One day God will judge evil people; they will burn up, and nothing will be left of them. But if we obey him, we will be free—free like young calves let out of a barn. So remember, trust the Lord and obey him. Obey him and live; disobey him and be destroyed!

CONCLUSION

So the *Old Testament* ends here, with the word "destruction" or "curse." The people are told to get ready for Elijah to come again. (Malachi 4:5) *Elijah* was John the Baptist. He was much like Elijah, a strange, powerful, fiery preacher. (See Matthew 11:14 and 17:10-13 in the *New Testament* where Jesus called John the Baptist "Elijah.")

Glossary

(Some terms used in *The Bible for Busy People*)

Aaron	Means *one who knows*. Moses' older brother, Aaron, was the first high priest in Israel.
Abraham	First, the Bible calls him Abram which means *high father*. God changed his name to Abraham, meaning *Father of Many*. He is the father of all believers (Galatians 3:29), the first patriarch.
Amalek	A warlike tribe of people who were always enemies of Israel, like Ammon and the Philistines. (See Psalm 83:7.)
Ammon	See *Moab and Ammon*.
Angel	A messenger from God. Usually when an angel appeared, whoever saw him would be terrified. (See Psalm 104:4 and Luke 1:11-13 and 30 in the *New Testament*.)
Anoint	To pour olive oil over someone's head. The oil was a sign that the person was being set apart as prophet or priest or king. The oil was also a symbol of the Spirit of God.
Anointed	See *Anoint*.
Apostle	A servant of Jesus who had God's authority. There were 12 apostles who preached God's message. They also wrote most of the *New Testament* scriptures.
Aram	Another name for the kingdom of Syria, north of Israel. Damascus was (and still is) its capital city.

Ark of the Covenant	See *Covenant Box.*
Artaxerxes	Son of Xerxes, King of Persia about 465-425 B.C. (Pronounced *arta-zerk-seez.*)
Assyria	A great and powerful kingdom in Messopotamia that ruled much of the world before 600 B.C. Nineveh was its capital city.
Asterisk	A star-like mark that tells you which words are in this glossary. It looks like this: *.
Avenger	The *avenger of blood* or *kinsman redeemer* was usually an older member of the family of the one killed. God gave him the right to kill the murderer. In fact, the whole family of the one killed could have that right. In the Bible, God and Jesus are the *real* avenger of blood. (See Romans 12:19 in the *New Testament*; see *kinsman redeemer* in this glossary.)
Babel	Means *gate of God.* Later called Babylon.
Babylon	A great city with huge high walls protecting it. Babylon ruled the world around 600 B.C. for a short time. Babylon is the great and powerful kingdom that finally destroyed Jerusalem and took most of its people into exile (about 586 B.C.). It was in southeastern Messopotamia, over 1,000 miles from Jerusalem.
B.C.	*Before Christ.* Actually, Christ has always lived with God, because he is God's son. "B.J." might be better, meaning "before Jesus was born."
Bethel	Means *house of God.* It is the place Jacob first dreamed of the ladder reaching up to heaven and the angels going up and down on it. Later Jacob called it *El Bethel* or *The God of Bethel.*
Bethlehem	Means *house of bread.* This little town was the birthplace of Jesus. It is called "the City of David," because David was also born there. It is just outside Jerusalem.

Birthright	In the old days the oldest son usually received the greatest amount of his father's property. (See Hebrews 12:16.)
Blessed	See *Blessing.*
Blessing	A promise that something good will happen in the future. Usually, it is connected with God's promises to Abraham. (See Genesis 12:1-3.)
Box	See *Covenant Box.*
Canaan	Another name for the promised land. (Today, it's called Palestine.) Canaan was Noah's son whose family settled in Palestine. Canaan could also refer to the people who lived in the land. Canaan was to be the home of all Israel. (Even today, many Israelites live in Canaan with the Arabs, their cousins. Abraham had Ishmael first, a slave's son. He is the father of the Arabs. Isaac, the free son, son of promise, is the father of the Jews [or Israel].)
Cherub	A giant and strange creature. It has wings, claws, hands, wheels, and four faces (bull, lion, eagle, and man). Others have just one face. God *rides* on these huge beings in the spirit world.
Christian	One who belongs to Jesus Christ. One who believes in Jesus and follows him.
Circumcision	To cut and remove the extra skin (or *foreskin*) from the penis of a boy or man. It was a sign of God's covenant between God and Abraham. (See Genesis 17.) To this day, circumcision is a common operation.
Cirrhosis	A disease that can destroy the liver.
Cistern	A deep hole to store water.

Cities of Refuge — Places of protection for those thought to have done wrong. There were no jails in Canaan. God's system of justice made every crime subject to an equal punishment: "Eye for eye; tooth for tooth; hand for hand; foot for foot." But if someone accidentally killed another person, he could go to a city of refuge to be protected from the family of the one he killed. The priests would have a trial there, and the man would either be freed, or he would be given over to the family of the one he killed. (See Numbers 35.)

Concubine — A slave wife who has no rights or property of her own. A slave who is treated as a wife. In the old days, it was considered okay to have slaves as wives. But unlike a real wife, concubines owned no property. Even their children belonged to the real wife, and not to the concubine. Solomon owned 300 of these. Solomon also had 700 wives. When he married so many, he disobeyed God's original plan—one man with one woman. (See Matthew 19:3-9 in the *New Testament*.) (Pronounced *konk-u-bine*.)

Context — The verses before and after a verse that give meaning and background to the passage.

Covenant — An agreement between two people or nations. A treaty. In the Bible it usually means the agreement between God and his people. Usually it was between a master (God) and a slave (man). (See also *Covenant Box*.)

Covenant Box — Also called *the ark of the covenant* or *the ark of the Lord*. It was a box containing three things: 1) Aaron's stick that had budded (Numbers 17:8); 2) the two stone tablets with the Ten Commandments written on them (Exodus 25:16 and Deuteronomy 10:2); and 3) a jar full of manna from the desert (Exodus 16:32-34). This holy box was a symbol of God's presence.

Cyrus	The King of Persia. Isaiah the prophet called Cyrus by name about 120 years before Cyrus' birth. He freed slaves from many nations. He let them return to their own countries.
Daniel	A great prophet who was in exile in Babylon with the prophet Ezekiel.
David	See *King David*.
Devoted	Committing all to God. Everything alive was killed and all wealth was given to God's worship.
Devotions	Personal Bible study and prayer. These are two of the most important ways we have of getting to know God. (See John 17 in the *New Testament*.)
Dice	See *urim* and *thummim*.
Dog	Not "man's best friend" as in America. In Israel, dogs ran in packs. They were dangerous pests, hated and feared. Perhaps they were like the wild dogs of Australia.
Edom	See *Esau*. Edom is the nation of which Esau was the father.
Edomites	See *Edom*.
Embalmed	In Egypt dead bodies were treated with certain spices. The bodies were kept from decomposing (rotting) for a long time. Part of the reason these bodies lasted so long was the dryness of the land.
Ephraim	Means *fruitful*. He was the second son of Joseph; he was born in Egypt. His tribe was a great tribe. After the kingdom of Israel split in two, the northern kingdom (Israel) was often called *Ephraim*.
Esau	Means *hairy*. Though he was older than Jacob, he lost his birthright. Jacob tricked him and Isaac their father out of the birthright. Esau's other name was Edom, meaning *red*. (See Genesis 27:35.)

Exile	When Babylon conquered Jerusalem, many of the Jews were made slaves and taken to Babylon. When Assyria conquered the northern kingdom of Israel, those Jews also went to Assyria as slaves. These times of slavery are referred to as "exile."
Faith	Believing or trusting in God. This is the way God accepts anyone as his friend. (See Romans 10:10 and Acts 10:43.)
Fast	To go without food. This, along with prayer, lets God know how serious we are about what we pray or about our work.
Fleece	The woolly coat of a sheep after it has been cut off (sheared).
Gallows	A pole used to kill people. Usually, a criminal would be nailed up on the pole or jammed down on the top of it. It was for public execution.
Genealogy	A list of names so the people of the old time could know their fathers' and grandfathers' and great grandfathers' names. It is like a family tree, going back many generations.
Gentiles	People who are not Jews.
Gospel	Means *good news*. The good news is that Jesus died for our sins, was buried, and was raised to life to make us right with God. See item 4 on page vi at the front of this book.
Habakkuk	Means *hugged*. Habakkuk was a very close friend to God.
Hebron	This town is mentioned in the Bible more than any other, except for Jerusalem. It is located about ten miles south of Jerusalem. This was Caleb's city; also it belonged to the priests as a city of refuge.
Hezekiah	A great and good king of Jerusalem and Judah. He ruled from about 725-695 B.C. Isaiah the prophet was his friend and helper.
High Priest	Leader of all the priests. Aaron was the first one.

Holiness, Holy	Means *different*, or *separate*: we must be different from the world and separate from the world in how we live. We must separate ourselves to God to be holy.
Household Idols	Also called *terephim*. Whoever had those "gods" got to inherit all the wealth in the family. That is why Rachel stole her father Laban's idols.
Intercede	To pray for someone. Jesus is on our side. He sits beside God the Father, speaking to God for us. He is like a lawyer for our defense before God.
Isaac	Isaac means *he laughs*. The son God gave Abraham, the son of God's promise to Abraham. When God told Abraham the second time he would have a son in one year, Abraham was ninety-nine years old. Both Abraham and his wife Sarah, age ninety, laughed at that! Isaac is the father of Jacob, who is the father of all the Israelites (Jews) in the world today.
Ishmael	The older son of Abraham who was born by Sarah's Egyptian slave, Hagar. He was not the promised son; he is the father of all the Arab nations in the world today.
Isaiah	Means *the Lord saves*. Isaiah was in the family of the kings of Jerusalem. He was the greatest writing prophet in the *Old Testament*.
Israel	Means *he wrestles with God*. Some say it means *Prince of God* or *he rules with God*. First it was Jacob's new name (see Genesis 32:28), then it was the name given to all his family and their children—the twelve tribes of Israel.
Jabbok	A stream of water that flows into the Jordan River about twenty miles north of the Dead Sea. This is where Jacob wrestled with God.

Jacob	Means *schemer, cheater, impostor,* or literally, *heel.* Throughout his life, Jacob was a con artist until God changed him. Then his name became *Israel,* which means, *he wrestles God.* (See Genesis 32:28 and 35:10.)
Jeremiah	Means *the Lord throws.* Jeremiah was called the *crying prophet.* He lived through the death of the Jewish state, when Jerusalem was destroyed by Babylon. We know more about his sad life than any other prophet in the *Old Testament.*
Job	May mean one who experiences anger or hostility, one who is mistreated. Job was an Arab chief who probably lived about the time of Abraham — around 2,100 B.C. (Pronounced *Jobe.*)
Joshua	Means *the Lord will save.* He became the leader of Israel when Moses died. Joshua led Israel into Canaan. (The name Joshua in Hebrew is the same name as "Jesus" in Greek.)
Judah	Means *praise* (he praises God) or *thanksgiving* (he thanks God). He was the son of Jacob who became father of the greatest tribe of Israel. His tribe settled in southern Palestine around Jerusalem. Jesus would be born from this tribe. (See Genesis 49:10.)
King David	David means *one who is loved.* He was "a man after God's own heart." He was a great king over the united land of Israel, and he was father of Solomon. In II Samuel 7:14 God promises David that Jesus Christ would be his "son" (about 1,000 years later).
Kinsman Redeemer	A kinsman redeemer was a male relative who was responsible to take care of family members. He was supposed to protect the family and to get revenge on any enemy that hurt a family member. In the Bible God and Jesus are called "kinsman redeemer" for us! (See also *Avenger.*)
Laban	Means *white* or *glorious.* Rebekah's brother, Rachel's father. He was as good a con artist as Jacob.

Lamentations	Another word for *crying*.
Leprosy	A dreaded disease that caused nerves to die and flesh to rot. There was no cure for it.
Leprous	See *Leprosy*.
Levites	Members of Levi's family. The men were priests for God.
Lord	Normally in this book there is no distinction between the names for God, calling them all *Lord*. But there *is* a difference. When "LORD" is capitalized all the way through in your Bible, it is God's personal name, which he gave to Moses from the burning bush. (See Exodus 3:13-15 for a description of this.) You can see the difference between "LORD" and "Lord" especially in Psalm 110:1. If you want to know more about the names for God, read the preface and introduction to your NIV Bible.
Malachi	Means *my messenger*. (Malachi may not even be a man's name.) Malachi is the last prophet of the *Old Testament*.
Manna	Means *what is it?* When the Israelites were in the desert, God fed them manna. They had never seen it before. It was left on the ground around their camp every morning, so they had to work every day to get it. It tasted sweet like honey cakes. (See Exodus 16:4-36.)
Marriage	Originally, God meant it to be one man with one woman. (See Matthew 19:3-9 in the *New Testament*.) The Bible says that God was married to Israel, and that Jesus is married to the Church. (See the book of Hosea in the *Old Testament*; see Ephesians 5:22-32 in the *New Testament*.)
Messopotamia	Means *between the rivers*. It is located between and near the Tigris and Euphrates Rivers. Abraham and his family were from there originally. (Map 1 and Map 2)

Midian	One of Abraham's sons by another woman, Keturah. (See Genesis 25:2-4.) His tribe lived east of the Jordan River, east of Israel. They were enemies of Israel.
Moab and Ammon	These were sons of Lot, Abraham's nephew; they were born to Lot's daughters by incest. (See Genesis 19:30ff.) His daughters got Lot drunk and had sex with him, so Moab and Ammon were born. (The Bible is very honest about sin.) Moab and Ammon became tribes that settled east of Israel, enemies of Israel.
Moabite	See *Moab*.
Moses	Means *taken out of water*. The princess of Egypt found Moses floating in a little boat, and she "took him out." Moses is the main writer of the first five books of the Bible—*The Pentateuch*. It was through Moses God gave the *Old Testament* law—the Ten Commandments.
Nahum	Means *comforter*. Nahum prophesied the fall of Nineveh.
Nazarite	One who belongs in a special way to the Lord. A Nazarite was a person who could not drink wine or cut his hair. (See Numbers 6:1-21.) (Samson was a Nazarite.)
Nebuchadnezzar	The great king of Babylon who conquered Jerusalem (about 600 B.C.) and the rest of the world then. Jeremiah, Ezekiel, Daniel, Habakkuk, and maybe others prophesied during Nebuchadnezzar's life. He was also called Nebuchadrezzar.
New Testament	First written in Greek, the *New Testament* is made up of the last 27 books of your Bible. These books and letters tell us about Jesus and the church. (See number 3 on page viii.)
Nineveh	The capital city of an evil empire, Assyria. It fell in 612 B.C.

Obed	Means *worshiper.* He was son of Boaz and Ruth, grandfather of King David.
Old Testament	The Jews call the *Old Testament* the "Hebrew Bible." These are the first 39 books of the Bible, written before Jesus was born.
Palestine	See *Canaan.*
Parable	These are simple stories that are to teach people the truth, or to hide the truth from some people. The parables may also be used as arguments against evil people.
Passover	God passed over the Israelite houses that had lamb's blood over their doors. God killed the oldest son in every Egyptian home. This is how Israel finally left Egypt. Also the name refers to a meal in celebration of this event, which is observed each year by Jewish families.
Pastor	Means *one who watches over.* A minister; a person who cares for sheep or for people.
Patriarch	Early father. In the Bible it means someone like Abraham, Isaac, Jacob, or Jacob's sons.
Pentateuch	The first five books of the Bible: Genesis, Exodus, Leviticus, Numbers, and Deuteronomy, believed to be written mainly by Moses.
Philistines	A warlike tribe of people who were always enemies of Israel. They lived on the plains along the coast of the Mediterranean Sea.
Poor	God made laws to provide for poor people. Rich people were to harvest their grain only once. Any grain that was left could be picked by poor people. God's welfare system was better than ours! The poor had to *work* to get food.
Priests	Men who were from Levi's tribe. (See Genesis 29:34 and then Numbers 1:47-53.) These Levites were the priests who were in charge of the worship of God.

	Priests pray to God and sacrifice to God and lead in worship for people.
Prophecy, Prophesy	To speak to people for God. Sometimes it is predicting the future, but usually it is simply giving a message to people for God. ("Prophecy" is a noun, Prophesy a verb.)
Prophet	One who speaks to people for God. True prophets were always 100% correct!
Proverbs	Short, wise sayings about life.
Psalm	Means *to play music and sing*. Psalms is the longest book in the *Old Testament*. It is a group of songs, hymns, prayers, and poems written by many different people. King David wrote many of the psalms. Psalms were used in the temple in Jerusalem for worship of God, a long time ago. (Pronounced *sahm*.)
Purim	Means *throwing dice* to choose the day Haman would have all the Jews killed. (See Esther 3:7.) It is a two-day feast or party the Jews have, even today, to celebrate not being killed by Haman. (Pronounced *poo-reem*.)
Redeem	Means *take or buy back*. (See *Kinsman Redeemer*.)
Refuge	See *Cities of Refuge*.
Remnant	What is left over. God always has *some* people who are truly his.
Repent	To be sorry and to change your behavior to do what is right.
Resurrection	Having died and then been raised by God to be alive. 1) A resurrected person never dies again. 2) Some people were raised from the dead back to this life again. They died again. (See John 11 in the *New Testament*.)
Sabbath	*Rest*. On the seventh day (the Sabbath) everyone in Israel was to rest. When God created the world in six days, he rested on the seventh day.

Sacrifice
: Something precious given to God. Your life, your mind and body, should be given to God to obey him only. That is *your* sacrifice. (See Romans 12:1 and 2.) In the *Old Testament* people killed animals for their sacrifice to God. (See Leviticus 1ff for example.)

Samson
: Means *sunny* or *little sunshine*. He was a judge who had God's power to be so strong, he was almost like superman! (See Judges 13-16.)

Samuel
: Means *God heard*. He was the first great prophet after the time of the judges. He anointed Israel's first two kings, Saul and David.

Scribe
: A lawyer who copied God's law. He also helped others to understand the law. During Jesus' life, many scribes became his enemies. (See Ezra 7:10.)

Sennacherib
: King of Assyria who attacked Jerusalem in about 702 B.C. His army was destroyed by God. Jerusalem was the only city in that part of the world that was left standing. (Pronounced *sin-'ak-er-ib*.)

Seraph
: Giant winged, fire-breathing dragons that always worship God in heaven. (See Isaiah 6:2f in the *Old Testament* and Revelation 4:7f in the *New Testament.*)

Sin, Sins
: (Means *missing the mark*; or *not hitting the bull's eye in a target*.) In the Bible sin is two things: 1) An *act*: a wrong or a mistake; breaking a rule or a law; rebelling against God or others; not doing what you know you should do; an error; going against what you know is right; wrong thinking or wanting what's wrong; rejecting Jesus or God. 2) A *fact*: something that lives inside us that we inherited from Adam through our parents. (See Romans 7:17-18 and I John 1:8.) This is with us as long as we are in the flesh, that is, until we die.

Solomon	Means *peace*. He was king of Israel after David. He was a great king, the wisest man who ever lived. He ruled for forty years. He is the man who wrote Proverbs, Ecclesiastes, and other parts of the *Old Testament*. He was the last king of all twelve tribes. After him the kingdom split in two.
Stocks	A wooden rack that kept a person from moving.
Tabernacle	A tent where worship of God was done by the priests. God gave exact measurements for its size and commands for its use and for moving it. (See Exodus 25-31 and 35-40 for the details.)
Terephim	See *Household Idols*.
Thummim	See *Urim and Thummim*.
Ur	The city where God first spoke to Abraham. It is located in southeastern Messopotamia on the Euphrates River near the Persian Gulf.
Urim and Thummim	Possibly animal bones kept in the clothing of the high priest. They were thrown into the priest's lap. Then the priest would tell what they meant. This is one way the people in the old days could tell what God wanted them to do. (See Proverbs 16:33.)
Vow	A promise made to God which must not be broken. (See Ecclesiastes 5:4 and 5.)
Wager	A bet. In Job, God bet that Job would be faithful no matter what happened. Satan bet that Job would reject God if bad things happened to Job. God was right, of course.
Xerxes	Also called Ahasuerus in the Bible. Xerxes was king of Persia from about 486 to 465 B.C. He is mentioned in the book of Ezra, Esther, and Daniel. (Pronounced *Zerk-seez*.)
Yoke	A bar and ropes that fit on a bull's neck when he pulls a cart.

Zechariah   Means *the Lord remembers*. (Pronounced *Zek-a-ri-ah*.)

Zephaniah   *The Lord hides* or *protects* or *treasures up*. Zephaniah told the people that God would judge them because of their sins.

Maps

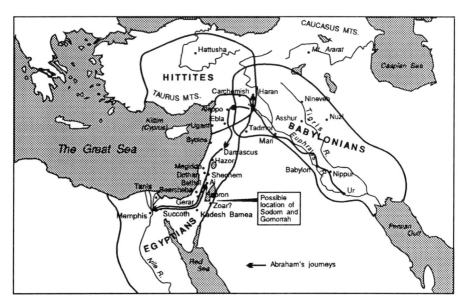

Time of the Patriarchs

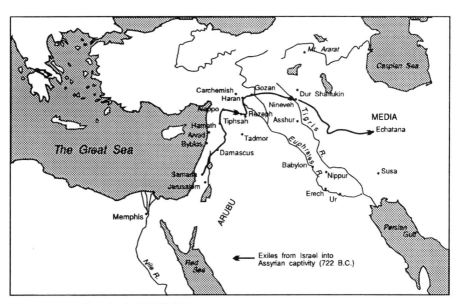

The Assyrian Empire (c. 700 B.C.)

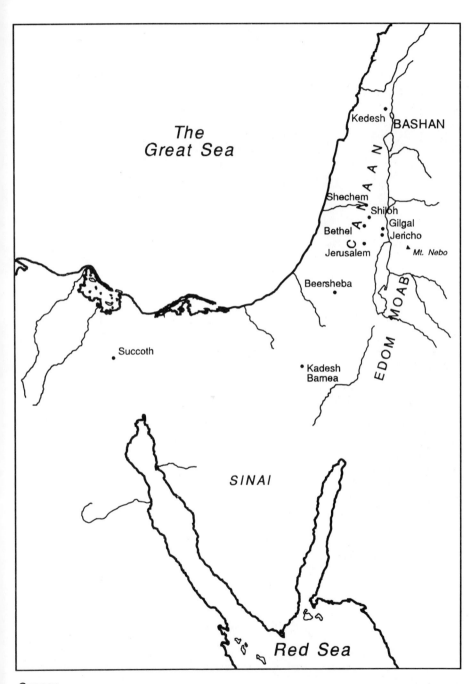

Canaan

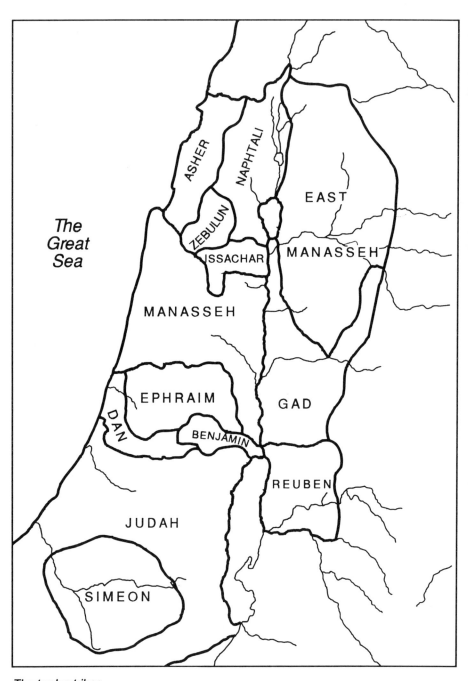

The twelve tribes

Index